More Than Bipolar

More Than Bipolar

A Memoir of Acceptance and Hope

Lizabeth D. Schuch

Lizabeth D. Schuch

iUniverse, Inc.
Bloomington

More Than Bipolar
A Memoir of Acceptance and Hope

The following names that appear in this book are pseudonymns:
Jenny, Billy, Don, John, Mark, Jeff, and Lisa.

iUniverse books may be ordered through booksellers or by contacting:

iUniverse
1663 Liberty Drive
Bloomington, IN 47403
www.iuniverse.com
1-800-Authors (1-800-288-4677)

ISBN: 978-1-4759-4980-3 (sc)
ISBN: 978-1-4759-4983-4 (e)
ISBN: 978-1-4759-4981-0 (dj)

Library of Congress Control Number: 2012916756

Printed in the United States of America

iUniverse rev. date: 10/24/2012

Praise for *More Than Bipolar: A Memoir of Acceptance and Hope*

"Lizabeth D. Schuch takes us on a rocky journey to recovery, educating readers about bipolar disorder, pinpointing flaws in our healthcare system, and inspiring us with her wit and determination to be much *More Than Bipolar.* A valuable book, fresh with insights."

—Pete Earley, author of *Crazy: A Father's Search Through America's Mental Health Madness*

More Than Bipolar chronicles a remarkable journey from illness to health, trials to triumphs, in the life of a brave young woman with a disease that is often underdiagnosed and mistreated. Bipolar disorder, commonly labeled manic depression, is not rare and is often attributed to life events that can morph into blaming oneself or others. It is a biomedical condition with a significant evidence base that can be effectively treated with medications. Nevertheless, we are not merely neurotransmitters, but unique individuals.

This is where Lizabeth Schuch has bravely allowed the reader to look into her personal experience of bipolar disease. She makes clear that it is not only important to receive an accurate diagnosis; it is equally important for physicians, family members, and other members of the person's extended environment to recognize the sum of who the person is with bipolar disorder, and not just associate the person with the disease itself. We come away from this wonderful autobiography recognizing there is treatment for bipolar disease and a successful future for all those affected by it.

Thomas N. Wise, MD
Professor of Psychiatry
Johns Hopkins University School of Medicine

A fascinating journey into Lizabeth's world of bipolar disorder episodes, hospital visits, and ultimately, healing. Her positive voice transcends the often harrowing, often humorous experiences of this disease, giving the reader insight into her powerful desire to be back in balance once again. Lizabeth is right. She is so much more than bipolar disorder. We all are!

—Julie A. Fast, author of *Loving Someone with Bipolar Disorder, Take Charge of Bipolar Disorder,* and *Get it Done When You're Depressed*

For Mom and Dad. Without your unconditional love, support, and belief in me, my life would have turned out quite differently. You gave me the foundation I needed to become who I am today. I love you both with all my heart.

We know that life is not always fair, easy, or what we might have planned; however, it is how we choose to respond to our circumstances that is perhaps the greatest determining factor for how our lives will ultimately turn out.

—*Lizabeth D. Schuch*

Contents

Foreword   xiii
Preface   xvii
Introduction: March 1, 1984   xxi

1. Growing Up: Prediagnosis   1

2. Life after the Olympics: Hospitalization #1   5

3. Credit Cards, Rental Cars, and Champagne Parties:
    Hospitalization #2   17

4. My Little Corner of Hell: Hospitalization #3   33

5. I Need a Time-Out: Hospitalization #4   47

6. The Golden Years: Life without Episodes   55

7. Opening Pandora's Box: Introduction to Depression   68

8. Beyond the Consultation: Psychiatry and Competent
    Treatment   84

9. Wanting the Pain to Go Away: Suicide   100

10. Believing What You Hear: Labels and Beliefs   110

11. Questioning Your Value: Internalizing Societal Stigma   123

12. Fearing Rejection: Dating Relationships   133

13. Sources of Strength: Supportive and Healthy Relationships   138

14. Family Connections: Genetic Predisposition   147

15. Maintaining Balance: Tips on Productive Living   155

Afterword: Where I Am Today   168
Appendix 1: Bipolar Disorder Explained   172
Appendix 2: Lithium   175
Notes   178
Resources   181
Acknowledgments   183

Foreword

BOOKS REPRESENTING PERSONAL STORIES of patients with bipolar disorder appear regularly today. But in many of these books, one would be hard-pressed to describe the person behind the bipolar illness as normal, the kind of person most of us would recognize among our family members, friends, and neighbors.

Not so for this book and its author, Lizabeth Schuch. Prior to the onset of her bipolar illness, vividly described in these pages, the author apparently led a reasonably happy and stable life—a life that might be described as normal. Indeed, even after the onset of her illness at the age of seventeen, the bulk of the life she describes is that of a well-adjusted woman succeeding and growing both professionally and personally.

Because the person described here is someone that the average reader can identify with and relate to, the descriptions of her episodes, and their impact on her and the people around her, are all the more powerful. In too many of the life stories of patients with bipolar illness, the chaotic drama of their lives—disrupted families, violence, sexual abuse, substance abuse—grab the reader's attention; the bipolar illness embedded in all of this can be difficult to appreciate. Not so with Lizabeth Schuch's story. Against the background of her normal life, the manifestations of her bipolar illness stand out for all to see.

The book opens with a description of her first manic episode and nicely characterizes the way in which it is often the patient who is the last to recognize that something is awry. There are no substance abuse issues, chaotic family members, or abusive hospital staff to distract the reader from her unfolding experience of a normal thought process evolving into the distortions of a psychosis.

Clearly Ms. Schuch's intention in writing this book goes well beyond the telling of a personal story, however dramatic and powerful it may be. Her mission is to educate the public. To pursue this mission, she has woven into the descriptions of her own illness a treasure trove of solid information about bipolar illness in general—suicide, substance abuse, the genetics of bipolar illness, how stress can trigger the onset of episodes, the importance of a supportive family, what makes a good psychiatrist, and the value of psychotherapy combined with medication are just a few of the topics she covers. Using her own story, she helps the reader appreciate that every bipolar patient must struggle with the temptation to adjust one's own medications or even to stop them, wisely concluding that the most successful treatment reflects a collaboration between doctor and patient. She describes what can happen when a bipolar patient encounters nonpsychiatric physicians who may not fully appreciate the importance of the bipolar medications.

The author poignantly describes the way in which society's negative attitudes about mental illness can become internalized in the insidious but powerful process of self-stigmatization, forming attitudes that can prolong the consequences of illness and retard recovery.

I am pleased that she has devoted a special section to the all too often forgotten drug lithium. It is a shame—indeed, it is inexcusable—that some psychiatrists have never really learned how to use lithium and feel "uncomfortable" with it. These are the psychiatrists who were trained since the early 1990s, when newer candidate mood stabilizers were developed. Because these new drugs had patent protection, the companies that developed them had the resources for substantial marketing and educational efforts, some of which aimed at convincing psychiatrists that a particular new drug was much better than lithium. Since lithium has always been a generic drug, it generates very little revenue, and accordingly there are precious few marketing or educational programs reminding clinicians of the continued importance of this drug—which was, after all, the first treatment shown to specifically treat bipolar illness. While the new drugs have certainly expanded the psychiatrist's ability to treat bipolar patients, the newer drugs have yet to show that they can fully replace lithium. They should be considered as alternatives or adjuncts to lithium rather than replacements for it.

Finally, I should point out that this book brings to life the reality that depressive episodes account for most of the toll that this illness takes from a life. Manic episodes are dramatic and can be quite disruptive, but it is the cumulative effect of the depressive episodes that requires the most perseverance, strength, and fortitude to continue to grow in spite of them. The author has done this. I also respect the fact that she never indulges in self-pity or a sense of being special because of her illness; one cannot say this about all bipolar memoirs.

It requires courage for a patient to write a book of this kind. For Ms. Schuch, an extra measure of courage is required precisely because she is a normal person in the real world. She is not a celebrity or otherwise famous. She is not a professional patient whose identity merges with the illness. She is not at the pinnacle of a career with nothing to fear from this kind of self-revelation. She wrote this book so that readers could get to know her and, through her, to know more about bipolar illness.

She has accomplished her goal. She trusts that the reader will be able to see her as a person as well as seeing the illness she struggles with, and she trusts that the reader will not conflate the two. I'm betting on her.

Frederick K. Goodwin, MD
Former Director, National Institute of Mental Health

Frederick K. Goodwin, MD, is Clinical Professor of Psychiatry at the George Washington University Medical Center. Dr. Goodwin conducts research on manic-depressive illness and engages in policy studies focusing on the impact of changing patterns of health care on quality and innovation in medicine.

Dr. Goodwin is the former Director of the National Institute of Mental Health (NIMH), the largest research and research training institution in the world. Prior to that, he held a Presidential appointment as head of the Alcohol, Drug Abuse, and Mental Health Administration.

A physician-scientist specializing in psychiatry and psychopharmacology, Dr. Goodwin is an internationally recognized authority in the research and treatment of major depression and manic-depressive illness. He was first to report the antidepressant effects of lithium in a controlled study.

The author of over 480 publications, Dr. Goodwin (with Kay Redfield Jamison, PhD) wrote Manic-Depressive Illness *and its second edition,* Manic-Depressive Illness: Bipolar Disorders and Recurrent Depression, *the latter of which was published in 2007. Both texts won national and international awards.*

Dr. Goodwin has also appeared on many national television shows including The Today Show, 20/20, 60 Minutes, The Charlie Rose Show, and Anderson Cooper 360, often to discuss current research and issues relating to depression and bipolar disorder.

Preface

MY LIFE TOOK AN unexpected turn in 1984. Although I felt like I was on top of the world, the world told me otherwise. I was a seventeen-year-old in the midst of a manic episode when a psychiatrist diagnosed me with manic-depressive illness (now commonly referred to as bipolar disorder). The term meant nothing to me. I was definitely not concerned about the future or how my life would be altered as a result of being diagnosed with this illness.

In that instant, my life changed forever.

Within hours of diagnosis, I was hospitalized in a psychiatric unit for one month. I was a fairly confident teen when I entered the hospital, but once I was stabilized and released, I stepped into a new world that now included mental illness. Although I was still under the illusion that I simply had an illness that needed to be treated so that I could move back to being normal again, new fears began to emerge. These fears were mostly about medications and side effects and how others would view me, because I experienced tremors and had difficulty concentrating (not to mention my odd behavior my schoolmates had witnessed). It was not until my second manic episode and hospitalization a year later that I began to comprehend the impact of a mental health diagnosis and what this illness would ultimately entail.

During the early years of diagnosis, with mood stabilization coming and going and two additional manias, my sense of self weakened. Without fully realizing it at the time, I internalized the negative beliefs about mental illness. I allowed the illness to rob aspects of my personality and my sense of self-worth. I felt branded by this illness and the negativity associated with it. I feared that if those around me knew about the illness, their perceptions of me would change. I transformed emotionally and struggled with the idea that I did not deserve good things. My sense of value was in doubt and ran counter to the person I felt like I was prior to diagnosis. I did not want any of my negative thoughts about being mentally ill to be true, and I tried to resist them the best I knew how.

My early goal was to regain some sense of normalcy, and to me this meant striving to be like everyone else. I always seemed to be behind my peers, and I worked so hard to just catch up. Not being where they were in life made me feel very different.

Between 1984 and 1990, I was hospitalized four times due to manic episodes. I refer to the decade of 1990 to 2000 (ages twenty-four to thirty-four) as my golden years, as those years were fairly effortless in the maintenance of my illness, with no manic episodes. However, in the fall of 2000 I experienced my first clinical depression, and ever since I have contended with a flux of clinical depressions as well as milder forms of depression compounded by the symptoms of seasonal affective disorder (SAD).

When I first began writing down my story in a notebook in 1990, I created a basic chapter structure and a narrative of my experiences, ending with my fourth hospitalization. Many with bipolar disorder have difficulty remembering the details of their manias; for me, the majority of my manic episodes are vivid. My thought at the time I began writing was to share with others what this illness looked like in order to create greater understanding and compassion. Fourteen years passed before I picked up my writing again, this time with the intention of it becoming an actual book. Now I was ready. I had come into my own and had experienced both extremes of the manias and depressions, and with my dedication to wellness, I had seen the successful results of my commitment. I could now address the full scope of this illness and its effects both physically and emotionally.

Although this book is my story of living with the illness, there is one chapter included where another person's story is shared. It is on the topic of suicide. I have not had personal experience with suicide, yet because it is a serious and frequent consequence of this illness, I wanted to be sure this subject matter was not ignored.

We often have no idea why something happens, but sometimes we are able to look back and find meaning in it. As I continued to work on sharing my twenty-five years of experience with this illness, my early thoughts concerned the risk I was taking in sharing everything with anyone who would read it, particularly those who knew me. Although difficult, exposing my vulnerabilities was the only way I knew to express what this illness can do to those who have it. As I neared completion, I surprisingly discovered how much the writing process informed me about myself and this illness. I found I was more readily sharing my bipolar experiences with others rather than keeping quiet about it—and I no longer feared their reaction as I had in the past. I have come to appreciate who I have become as a result of this illness, which is a combination of a more empathetic, compassionate, and balanced person. My illness enabled me to have increased sensitivity for many people in today's world where mood disorders are so prevalent.

The reality of the continuing need to adapt to this illness is what I believe accounts for my ability to gain the upper hand and to not allow this illness to control or define me. My desire to respond to the diagnosis of bipolar disorder with diligent care is what has played a role in shaping who I have become.

Gaining a more mature understanding of what I had always believed to be true—that this illness is not the sum of who I am—is now my grounding, a strong foundation from which to move forward. Although managing this illness is essential, defining myself by it is not.

Mental illness has been around since the beginning of time, and it does not discriminate. Bipolar disorder is an illness of the brain, and it can happen to anyone. It is the way I chose to respond to this illness—its challenges and the suffering—that has made the difference for me. I recognize and respect that many with this illness have experienced much worse and do not have access to resources, treatment, and support. Many others are not diagnosed as quickly as I was, which accelerated my opportunities for effective treatment. The advantage of early and accurate diagnosis is that it has the potential to change the quality of treatment and success rate immensely.

Acceptance and adherence (also referred to as compliance) in regard to this illness are two words that resonate well with me: acceptance that I had this illness and adherence to medication and psychiatry appointments occurred immediately for me. Next came commitment to incorporating lifestyle changes that would support my health and well-being. Living with a mental illness is markedly different with all the necessary requirements to regulate daily living, particularly when taking into consideration routine life stressors that also need to be addressed.

It did take time to learn new coping skills that are a part of living a productive life with bipolar disorder. These coping skills developed into a way of life that allowed me to be both balanced and committed to wellness. Dedication to health and self are integral for me. I feel confident in my abilities to manage this illness with consistency. I do not take my health for granted; it is a result of the effort I put into it. My attitude regarding my own welfare is paramount. I consistently work to educate myself and stay on top of research. Knowledge is definitely powerful and has enhanced not only my relationships with psychiatrists to achieve optimal treatment, but also how I view myself.

What I wanted desperately to believe in the beginning—and what has shown itself to be true—is that I have always had within me the capacity and power to live a productive, happy, and fulfilling life.

Introduction
March 1, 1984

IT'S SEVEN O'CLOCK IN the evening on a school night. My parents tell me we're going out to see a doctor. I immediately run to my room and start throwing items into an overnight bag. I know there is more to this trip, and we must be going somewhere good—I can just feel it. I throw in my swimsuit because I'm quite sure my training for the summer Olympics in Los Angeles is part of the excursion.

My enthusiasm abruptly changes to agitation. I sit on the top of the stairs outside my bedroom and state with certainty, "I'm not going." My mom and I struggle back and forth, and then I just as abruptly give in and say, "Okay." I'm back to feeling excited again. I can't wait to get on our way to wherever we are going.

My mom, dad, and I get in the car, and we first stop off at the high school to pick up my purse, which I had left behind at school that day. I don't even care that I left behind something so important; I can't be bothered with something so insignificant at this moment. I do notice that they keep the child locks on in the backseat where I'm sitting, while one of them runs in. I'm not sure why they would do that. I'm not going anywhere—I'm thrilled to be on this adventure.

We arrive at an office building and meet Dr. A. My parents tell me he is a psychiatrist. I've never met a psychiatrist before, but that's okay. He is very nice and begins to ask me questions. I stop him and ask, "Where's the couch? Isn't there supposed to be a couch?" I ask if I can squish down in the chair I'm sitting in, with my legs extended as if to mimic some sort of couch position. He says that will be fine, and now I am more comfortable.

After what seems to be about ten minutes of questions, Dr. A. says to me, "Lizabeth, you are a textbook case manic-depressive."

I say, "Okay," but I don't have a clue what that means, and I don't really care—it's all fine with me. I'm in my own world and am not really hearing him. He then talks directly to my parents, and soon we are in the car again, off to a hospital that seems to be far away.

It's dark out, and everything seems to be flying by as I peer out the window. The lights and buildings and more lights zoom by; it feels like we are going really, really fast. I'm talking nonstop, and it's hard to even take a breath because I have so much to say. I haven't received more than an "Uh huh" or an "Okay" from Mom and Dad. It's odd that they are not joining in with me in all my great observations.

Even though they say we're going to a hospital, I know that there is some hidden meaning in it all. This whole day has been very cryptic, but I know that wherever we're going and whatever the reason, this is all about me and it's all for me, so it must be all great stuff. I've got my swimsuit with me, and I will be able to continue my Olympic training, so that's all that really matters for now.

We enter the lobby of a hospital I've never been to or seen before. My mom sits down, and she cannot seem to stop crying. I don't know what's wrong; I'm having such a great time, so why would she be crying? The fleeting thought of wondering why escapes me very quickly. My dad suggests we go into the hospital chapel. We pray and wait … and wait … and wait. Finally the staff tells us there is a room ready for me, and I'm feeling hopeful that this new adventure is going to get rolling. There are no rooms available on the open unit, so I will have to stay in the closed unit. I don't really know what that means; all I care about is that I smell chlorine, and I know we must be at the right place; the pool has got to be somewhere close by.

Before I'm allowed to go to my room, someone goes through my personal belongings. They take everything sharp, including my blush (which has a mirror in the case), and then they take my shoelaces from my running shoes. I don't really get that, but whatever, I just go along with it all.

The staff takes the three of us to a floor in the hospital, and we enter through some large double doors. It's very late now. We walk into an area with about six rooms in a horseshoe shape. There is someone sitting at a desk on my left as I walk in. The carpet is green, kind of like a golf course. My parents see me in and help me get settled into what I'm told is my room, and then they have to say good-bye. They seem sad, but really it's okay. I know this is where I'm supposed to be. It's all part of a great big plan, and it's all for me.

I know I'm supposed to go to bed, but I just can't sleep—too much excitement to sleep. Sleep is kind of a waste of time, anyway. I get up and walk out of my room into the main area. It's quiet and dark, and I'm told to go back to my room, to sleep. I get into bed but don't really sleep at all. In what seems to be the very early morning, a vampire comes into my room while I'm still in bed and draws my blood. Then a psychiatrist comes to my room and starts asking a lot of questions. He tells me the nurse will be giving me some pills. She hands them to me. I take them. I always do what doctors tell me to do.

Now it's daytime, and I can actually see what's going on. There are other people with rooms of their own in the same corridor. I wander over to the large doors where I came through last night. There are two narrow windows above the door handles. As I peer out, I can see other rooms along a very long hall and more people. I'm really not all that interested; for now I'm just waiting for the next cue as to where this adventure will be taking me. I know there is something planned for me—something good.

I am introduced to a woman sitting in a rocking chair. She looks familiar. She has on a blue sweatshirt with "Physical" scrawled across the front. I love that song by Olivia Newton-John. Well, her hair is blonde, and it looks like it really could be … yes, I think it's *actually* Olivia Newton-John. When we're introduced, she says her name is Jenny. Okay, so she's using a different name; it doesn't really matter. She seems to take a liking to me. She's older than me and takes me under her wing. Very early in our conversation, she tells me we are making a movie. "A movie? Wow, this is great!" It makes total sense that someone would want to make a movie with me in it, and now this explains why I'm in this place. How fun is this! I soon get nervous about the cameras being on at all times, and I ask her what to do when I'm in the shower. She tells me not to worry and to just close my eyes, and they will stop the filming. Whew, what a relief! I like walking around this place knowing we are filming with those hidden cameras, and I have a lot of fun with it. It feels great to be a star!

It's now my second night here, and it's late again. I find it's still hard to sleep. Just like last night, I wander out to the horseshoe-shaped area and start talking to the kid sitting at the tall desk by the door; he's doing his homework and tells me he's in college. After a little while he also tells me I need to go back and try to go to sleep. I say okay.

As I turn around to walk toward my room, I see a vision of two people in one of the rooms behind their closed doors. Something in me knows that what I'm seeing is not real. Weird. I just keep walking and wander back into my room. In no time I'm up again and go back out to talk to the kid doing his homework. Nice guy, but apparently he has a job to do, and he tells me very gently that I really need to try to sleep. I try, but it's not really working. They tell me they will give me something to help. At last I am in la la land for a few hours.

After taking those pills for a couple days, things start getting fuzzy, and I start slowing down. I begin to realize that I'm not feeling normal. Also, I notice that without a code, those big double doors don't open and close. It does not faze me; we are in here to make a movie, and that's what's important.

My mom visits me every day and brings me a McDonald's vanilla milkshake and fries each visit. I love those vanilla milkshakes! I love my mom visiting and the special attention I get. However, one day she makes me so mad that I tell her I hate her, and she leaves in tears. After she's gone, I can't remember why I got so angry. She's the best. I'm not mad anymore.

I continue to wear my brand-new running shoes that I wore in here. They are kind of a pinkish-red color. I love these shoes! I went out for the track team just before coming in here, and I knew I would need them. Of course they took out my shoelaces for some crazy reason, but I still walk and run around in them all the time—why not? I certainly don't have any desire to wear slippers, like some of the others.

I'm having a great time in here. Jenny uses the pay phone in the unit and orders us a pizza. Cool! It's just about then that I realize there are rules in this place. Ordering a pizza to be delivered to what they call a closed unit is not okay. We laugh when we find out we broke the rules, and the nurses let us keep it anyway.

Jenny and I talk and talk, until one day she up and snaps at me and suddenly gets very mean. I cry and cannot understand, because she said she liked me so much. A nurse comforts me and explains that she is sick too, and I should not take it personally.

Hmm ... the nurse said, "She's sick *too*." It's been about four days since I arrived here, and I'm starting to wonder if I'm here for a reason other than the movie. I'm getting really confused, and the doctor does not seem to think there really is a movie being made. I don't want to believe him. He can't be right, can he? What is going on?

There is a boy who waves to me through the narrow windows of the very large double doors. I find out his name is Billy, and he seems close to my age. I am told that he and I are the only young ones here, and he has no one else to relate to. He looks kind of sad and lonely. He comes by often, but he's on the other side, so we cannot talk. Somehow we seem to bond without speaking.

Two days later I'm on the same side of the doors as Billy. I still have a private room, and I still think we're making a movie. Jenny is left behind the double doors.

Chapter 1
Growing Up: Prediagnosis

I WAS BORN IN a small suburb south of Chicago called Homewood, Illinois, in 1966. I have three siblings: Debbie, Douglas, and Susanne. I am the second eldest, after Debbie. We have a very small extended family. My mom has one sister, and my dad has one brother. My aunt and uncle each have two children, for a total of four first cousins.

My childhood memories are very fond and are filled with family and friends. My relationship with my parents was loving and supportive, and both were emotionally and physically present. We were a tight-knit family who spent much time together. My three siblings and I got along just fine, and there was closeness among us. I'm quite sure I was blessed with a better than average childhood. As with any one person's life, there certainly were good and bad times.

We were also very close with both sets of grandparents. Grandma and Grandpa Schuch lived in a tiny town in Michigan called Sawyer. My grandfather was a butcher, and they owned a meat market, which was next door to their home. Many happy memories were created there, and all four of us children loved visiting them.

My mother was born in Sweden and came with her parents to the United States when she was eleven. Grandma and Grandpa Peterson lived outside Chicago, and as young children we spent a lot of time with them as well.

Due to my father's employment, we moved three times throughout my childhood and adolescence. He made his career with US Steel and stayed with them until he retired after thirty-six years of service. He was transferred from Chicago to a suburb of Pittsburgh, Upper St. Clair, when I was seven. I was not really that upset about moving; it was a change that was kind of exciting to me. We lived there for two and a half years. Life continued to go smoothly, and before I knew it, Dad was transferred again. This time we were off to Birmingham, Alabama—known as the "Pittsburgh of the South" (because of US Steel's presence). I was now in the fourth grade.

It was somewhat overwhelming and a little sad to move this time, yet once again I felt a bit of excitement. Vestavia Hills, Alabama, agreed with me. By eighth grade I was very well adjusted to living in the South and was as happy as could be. I certainly enjoyed the weather and having access to the warm sun for longer periods throughout the year, as compared to when I lived in Pittsburgh. One of my favorite family memories was spending time together boating, water skiing, and swimming at Smith Lake, where we went one day of each weekend during the summer. Life was good.

I continued to be blessed in so many ways. I became involved with my church youth group and choir, girl scouts, softball, swimming, piano, and babysitting. My life was very active, and I was happy doing the things I wanted to do. I had many friends and spent much time with them. I was so happy, what could possibly go wrong?

Then it happened again: my dad was transferred, and we moved back to Upper St. Clair in October of 1979. Although this area may have been familiar to the family, this move devastated me. I was in the middle of eighth grade and was thirteen years old. I not only loved Birmingham for the people but also for the warm climate. Now we would be going back to cold, dreary Pittsburgh. I cried until I could cry no more. Three separate groups of friends held going-away parties for me, and I did not want to leave. Tough as it was, did I have a choice? Obviously not—I was just a kid and had to go along with my family.

Needless to say, at first I hated living in Pittsburgh again, and I found myself crying several times a week. After school all I did was write letters to my friends in Birmingham. People in the neighborhood would ask me to come outside to hang out, and I refused. I entered into a school where students had already been together for several years, and I was a complete stranger to most. Students ridiculed me for having lived in the South; I was called the "Alabamian illiterate" by one boy, and others made fun of me too. As a thirteen-year-old, this was hurtful and personal. I really don't think they had a clue about what the Deep South was like in the late 1970s. Would you believe that some wanted to know what it was like to have slaves and go barefoot to school? What made the teasing worse was that I was an extremely sensitive person and took it all to heart. I even cried in school. This was the first time I recall feeling judged and isolated, and my response was sadness. With the girls, I moved from clique to clique until one finally accepted me. Apparently, at my new school that was the way it was. I saw others go through the same process after me, but that did not make it any easier. As I look back, I think this could possibly have been my first experience with some form of depression, although it was situational in nature. It also occurred in the fall, and that is perhaps a key factor when looking back at patterns that have formed with my illness and how seasonal changes play a role.

I experienced the ups and downs of a typical teenager, and my confidence would sometimes waver. My perfectionist personality ran my self-image regarding how I looked to myself. I was always concerned about my weight, even though at worst I was probably five pounds overweight. I was always trying to achieve that perfect weight. I also recall never being satisfied with the way I looked, particularly my hair. I was often in the bathroom trying to fix it, or I had to pass the bathroom up altogether because I did not want to see myself in the mirror; I felt I never looked good enough.

I often compared myself to my older sister and younger brother as far as academics were concerned. I was two years behind Debbie in school, and she was always the model student. Debbie was extremely bright and went on to Duke University after she graduated. My brother, on the other hand, was two years younger than me, and he was doing college math in high school; he even got a perfect score on the math section of the SATs. Come on, who does that? He also went to Duke. I always thought I was the average one stuck between them.

As I grew up, there were already a few things that stood out and made me feel different. First off, I was left-handed. Although at times I felt it was kind of cool because I was often the only one in a group who was not right-handed (and that made me feel kind of special), at the same time I was not like the other kids, and many things were not geared for lefties, such as scissors, spiral-bound notebooks, and pencil sharpeners. Also, my name is spelled differently because it does not have an "E" in the front; all my life I have had to explain that, and to this day I am still often called Elizabeth. Although I love my name and people have often told me how neat my name is, once again this made me feel different in my early teens.

Thankfully, things did get better. Before I knew it, it was time for high school to start. This was where I met my real friends, and I became involved in activities again. I joined choir, made the volleyball team, became involved in church, and skied (this time downhill). For my last three years of high school, I was in the color guard. I was also in the spring musical my junior and senior years. I sold Avon and continued to babysit. I always enjoyed working and having my own money. I liked the independence and responsibility associated with it; that was important to me.

One of the myths specifically verbalized to me about about manic-depressive illness back in the mid-1980s was how a dysfunctional environment affects people with this illness. This misconception—that an emotionally traumatic experience as a child later manifests itself into some form of bipolar disorder—only adds to the confusion about the truth of the illness. Although this may be the case, it is not a determinant risk factor. Triggers for the onset of bipolar disorder can be as specific as medication-induced, or something much less specific, such as an environmental factor (a distressing event). What I do know is that there is a genetic predisposition for bipolar disorder, but for me, there was no traumatic childhood incident.

Chapter 2
Life after the Olympics: Hospitalization #1

SENIOR YEAR IN HIGH school was where it all really began. What was supposed to be the last few months leading up to the end of my senior year—full of anticipation for prom, graduation, college, and exciting times—instead resulted in a mixture of overwhelming and extreme levels of elation, embarrassment, anger, irritability, sadness, and loneliness.

Aside from having a genetic component, there is often a trigger of some kind that prompts the initial onset of a mania or depression, which results in the full-blown manifestation of bipolar disorder. Although the following is an account of my trigger, my purpose is not to place blame here. To me, understanding what I believe turned out to be the triggering event that led to the initial manic episode is very important for being aware of stressors that would later trigger other manic episodes. I feel that many things have to be in line for bipolar disorder to be triggered: time of year, age, maturity level, ability to respond to stressful situations, and emotional vulnerability level. I believe this one event alone did not put me into a manic state.

In February of 1984, at age seventeen, I was out of town traveling with a family to babysit their young daughter. I was very close to their family. One day while at the beach, her mother told me I could stay out in the sun a little longer and said she would start getting her daughter showered and ready. (This was my job and part of the reason I was there.) I looked to the dad as a father figure, and he seemed about the same age as my own dad. He was very fair skinned and was really burning in the sun. I mentioned this to him, as I would to my own father. His friend (with whom we were staying) instructed me to go inside and get him a shirt, which I immediately did. When I walked in the bedroom, the mother very quickly asked me what I was doing. When I explained, she told me that I was there to take care of her daughter, *not* her husband. With the way she said it, I thought she was implying that I had feelings for her husband. I was shocked and sickened that she could even have had that thought. I was an emotional wreck, and it all hit me in an unbelievable way. I cried and I remember calling my mom and wanting to leave. I did not know what to do.

Later that evening while the little girl's parents were out to dinner, the homeowner's wife was quite mean to me because I spilled some cereal in the kitchen. When the parents came home from dinner, they found me scrubbing the entire kitchen floor. While they were not totally surprised by the woman's reaction to what they thought was a minor mishap, they were puzzled as to why I would go to the extreme that I did to clean the whole floor.

I recall going out by the pool in the dark and crying for what seemed like hours on end. I was confused and upset; I had just been scolded by a woman I barely knew, but because I was a guest in her home, I did not want to upset her more than I already had. This was compounded by the notion that the little girl's mom thought I had feelings for her husband (much later I found out that the mother had not thought this, but she had reacted the way she did for reasons I would have had no way of knowing). The result of the way I felt was that I had an emotional breakdown. I was seventeen, sensitive, and maybe at a fragile place.

For the remaining days of the trip, I was waxing and waning between the onset of mania coupled with periods of normalcy. The day after my emotional breakdown, the little girl said something that surprised me, coming from a seven-year-old. As we were walking along the beach, she looked at the shells and said to them, "I'm sorry we cannot pick up all of you, but you are all beautiful in your own way." I then began to see a parallel between people and seashells and how beautiful each and every one of us is, but that does not mean we can like (or keep) each one. I took her childlike idea literally and collected probably one hundred seashells, taking all of them home to shellac and give away as gifts. I thought I would be giving some sort of extension of me. Also, while on that same beach, I started doing all kinds of cartwheels and backbends on the sand. I'm sure one could think I was just playing with the little girl, but it really was a bit excessive.

On the plane ride home, the little girl and I were mimicking all kinds of different accents, and I would not give it a rest. Again, one could think I was simply playing along with her, but I think even she was getting tired of it.

The following week, new behaviors started showing up, especially at school. I was going nonstop with very little sleep. I exercised like crazy and even went out for the track team, although I had never had an interest in it before or ever considered whether or not I even had the potential to be a decent runner. I did not just think I was good—I *knew* I was good. I was not eating enough, was definitely at an all-time low in weight, and thought I looked and felt the best I ever had.

I was also continuing to talk a lot and very fast. I was in the high school musical, and at rehearsal I simply would not stop talking. I kept going on and on about things that were not making sense to anyone else. I recall my friend Andrea slapping me across the face as I continued nonstop. Andrea remembers the situation as if something was possessing my thoughts, and the slap was an attempt to snap me out of it. At that moment I did not understand why she was reacting that way; I was not angry, just a bit confused. Others were shocked with her response, but she really did not know what else to do. I guess no one really understood what was going on. Meanwhile, I was just as happy as could be. The whole scene of her slapping me—as well as other friends becoming increasingly confused and frustrated with me—did not faze me; I was feeling very high on life, and nothing could touch me.

I was taking calculus and began solving math problems in a very interesting way. (If you ever saw the film *A Beautiful Mind* and remember the chalkboard and how nothing was really making sense, this is exactly what was going on with me. Both are forms of psychosis.) My calculus teacher even said to me, "Lizabeth, you have created new math!" I'm sure he did not know what the heck was going on. I, in turn, took what he meant to be a personal stroke of genius.

While participating in gym class, a male classmate picked me up, turned me upside down, and spun me around. I did not try to stop it but just laughed and had fun with it. Going along with it went hand-in-hand with my manic state at the time. Normally I was a person who always wanted to act appropriately, and I would have probably been embarrassed by the whole thing instead of enjoying it as I did.

That same day, I was busy handing out the many seashells I had picked up in Florida and shellacked in our basement. Although I can't remember specifics, I recall giving away some other random items of mine. I had also brought an old camera of my dad's from the 1960s to school, and I took lots of pictures; I guess I was suddenly going to become a photographer. I recall one classmate being afraid that I was going to commit suicide. I never really understood that and what it had to do with the camera, because harming myself would have been the last thing I would have wanted to do, unless he thought it was some way of saying good-bye (and perhaps he saw me giving things away). I also heard that some students thought I was on drugs. They just did not understand—and how could they? All that I knew was that I still felt I was pretty much the greatest thing since sliced bread, and I paid no attention to what anyone else said.

My friends were scared of my new changes in behavior, and understandably so. They had never seen anything like this. One friend thought my behavior had something to do with a Christian camp I had been to for a week that past summer (at least eight months prior). My friends were just searching for something on which to blame my new behavior. They were probably grasping at straws to come up with anything possible that had gone on in my life over that past year or so, and I certainly don't blame them.

Things were getting out of hand in so many different ways, and it was clearly affecting all aspects of my life. I was not sleeping more than a few hours a night, but I had an abundance of energy. My thoughts were racing. Even the television seemed to be talking to me directly—as if the person on TV could actually see me, and the ad or message was being delivered specifically to me.

Although I have never tried it, I have been told that being manic is similar to the appealing effects of cocaine: the feelings of invincibility, grandiosity, and elation. To be told these feelings are "not right" is virtually impossible to accept during the high of a manic episode. (These were the effects I felt during my first mania, yet they are certainly not the only ones possible, and everyone has their own experience that can vary from episode to episode.)

Everything came to an abrupt halt when I skipped a class to go swimming. Skipping class was another thing I had never done before. I remember thinking I did not care and maybe was a little tired of doing the right thing when I knew others were not always following the rules. I've always had a great love for water, and swimming has been a big part of my life. The year was 1984, and the summer Olympics were ahead—and yes, somehow I thought I was going, and *not* as a spectator. As I finished a lap, one of our school police officers was there to get my attention and said that my mom was in the guidance counselor's office, and I needed to go join her there. I immediately complied without question. I did not completely dry off and came into the office clothed, yet sopping wet. Apparently the school had taken notice of my odd behavior and called my mom. When I sat down to meet with my mom and the counselor, this was perhaps my first moment to be still and just breathe. I was feeling out of it but was not feeling high at this point. I was still very confused and did not understand what was going on. The counselor asked me if I knew why they had called me to her office. My response was, "I need help." I knew this was not what I was really thinking, but my answer was what an inner voice in my head was telling me I was supposed to say. In actuality, I thought I was better than fine.

After this, things moved rather quickly. Fortunately for all of us, my brother had a high school friend whose father was a psychiatrist with a very good reputation. Upon our return home from the counselor's office, my parents contacted this psychiatrist and set up some sort of emergency appointment. The psychiatrist was willing to see us that evening. (He could have just as easily urged us to go straight to the emergency room, and had this happened, my assessment and treatment protocol may have turned out very differently.)

My parents were very worried and did not know exactly what was going on with their daughter. I, on the other hand, was back to being very high and excited, wondering where this little adventure to the doctor was going to take us. I also experienced some abrupt variations in mood that evening, because my initial willingness to go to the appointment (to the extent of packing an overnight bag in anticipation) was suddenly replaced by irritable resistance, only to rapidly shift back to excitement again.

The appointment itself was brief, and aside from my disappointment that there was no couch to lie down on (like I had seen on television), it was pretty uneventful for me. The doctor quickly determined what the problem was and diagnosed me with manic depression; it didn't seem like there was any question about that. After he finished speaking with me, he spoke with my parents. Then he arranged for me to be admitted into the psychiatric unit at Jefferson Hospital, about thirty minutes away. I did not really understand all that was going on, but it seemed like something fun was in the works.

With my overnight bag in hand, I was prepared. I truly had a strong sense that I was going somewhere that evening that would require extra clothes. My ability to sense things like this would continue with my subsequent manic episodes: everything would seem to be connected to the next thing, as if there were some big plan in place, and it always was something good that was going to have an impact on me. I was off for an adventure and trying to make sure they had a swimming pool, as I needed to prepare for the Olympics.

While in the hospital waiting room, I could neither sit still nor shut up. Dad looked worried and Mom was crying. My dad and I then went into the hospital chapel and read from the Bible. We prayed together and it was quite emotional. I really felt God's presence with us. While we were reading, it was as if the word of God was being spoken directly by God through us. It was wild.

After what felt like hours, it was finally time for things to get moving again. Someone took me into a room where they went through everything I was wearing and stripped me of all my items of value as well as anything I could potentially use to try to harm myself or others. I couldn't help thinking that this was what it was like to be searched when going to jail.

It was now finally time to go to the room they had prepared for me. I was told that I would be placed in the closed (or locked) unit. I could have cared less. I just wanted to get the show on the road!

I was unable to sleep the first few nights. This made the days very long. Even when a doctor gave me some pills to take, nothing seemed to help the insomnia. I initially had some brief visual hallucinations, which I had not experienced prior to going into the hospital; I had had racing thoughts and grandiose ideas, but not hallucinations. The lack of sleep may have contributed to the hallucinations.

There were only five other patients on this closed unit, and aside from the fact that I was not fully aware of what was going on, I made a couple new friends and actually enjoyed myself in there. I had not yet grasped the notion that everyone, including me, was there for some sort of problem.

The hospital adventure began to slow down once the doctors started administering various psychotropic medications to discover the best combination for me. The medications doped me up and made me feel spacey and out of it. I experienced unsettling side effects, including extreme tremors and nausea. Over time I definitely became aware that I was not myself and was very confused.

Within a week, it was time to leave the closed unit to go down the hall to the open unit. There were only two of us on that whole floor of this thirty-six-bed inpatient psychiatric unit who were under the age of twenty. In fact, the two of us were considerably younger than the rest. I was beginning to stabilize: the mania had faded, and the confusion was starting to lift. As the mania went away, so too did my belief that I was part of an ongoing movie. The notion that I was training for the Olympics was gone, too. The drugs had really kicked in fast thanks to all the medications they had me on (although I still continued to experience many side effects and walked around in a fog some of the day). But by no means was I back to my old self.

As was true to form for me, once I was out on that open unit, I became very involved in the activities made available to us, although I was initially reluctant to participate. Getting used to hospitalization, realizing that something is wrong with you, being medicated, and experiencing strange side effects left many patients wanting to be alone. However, on the open unit, a significant component of the recovery process required occupational therapy, recreational games, crafts, and more. With all the new medications, my concentration was poor, and I became impatient with myself. I remember doing ceramics and trying to paint. My hands were shaking from the tremors caused by lithium. It was so frustrating that I wanted to quit. I felt like I was at a third or fourth grade level; I could not read for very long, and all my craft projects took a long time to make.

The structured program at this hospital kept me busy, and I did not have a chance to get bored or think of other things; perhaps this was the whole idea. It was at this hospital where I learned to play pool. The older male patients taught me, and I loved it and grew to be pretty decent at it.

After I was a little more adjusted, I became involved in every outside activity made available to us: movies, shopping area visits, walks, and trips to the botanical gardens at Phipps Conservatory. I always thought it was kind of odd, all of us walking around with our hospital ID bracelets. If anyone noticed, would they realize we were part of a mental wing of a hospital? At least we had jackets on that covered up the bracelets most of the time. I thought the whole thing was kind of peculiar.

I seemed to be the only truly manic person on the floor, keeping as busy as I did. The interesting thing I see now, looking back, is that this mania seems to be an extension of my true personality. Even as I was brought back to reality, I was still very upbeat, and the other patients found my personality very refreshing. The patients told me I was able to make others happy without trying.

The other patients on my floor were the best part of my stay. Because we all experienced some form of a mood disorder, they were so much like me, except they were older. We basically lived together 24/7, and we began to see one another as friends and an extended family. No wonder I enjoyed the hospital: everyone was so nice and seemed to like me. I loved receiving lots of attention, and not only from the patients; I grew to like the fact that a doctor would come to see me every day, along with nurses, family, and visitors. Also, no one wanted to hurt me or make fun of me. No one cared about what I wore or how I looked. I was totally accepted, and it was a nice feeling to be treated in that manner. I also did not really care what anyone thought of me in there, which was contradictory to how I often felt in high school.

Another contributing factor to my recovery from this initial episode was the outpouring of compassion I received from family and friends, from church and school. People called, sent cards and letters, and visited. My mom's daily visits were something to which I always looked forward; her love and dedication meant so much to me, and I'm not sure what I would have done without her. My dad would come too, but of course he had to work and be there for my younger siblings. My younger sister remembers coming with my mom and bringing her homework. The overall feeling of being loved, supported, and not judged was huge for me.

Having such a strong support system was what also enabled me to quickly get the help I needed. The time frame of when I began getting manic until the time I was diagnosed was between a week to ten days, including the beach trip. To me this seems to be a very short time, and I am thankful that my behavior did not get more out of control.

During this first manic episode, I felt great; it was those around me who suffered. This experience was very stressful on my family, particularly on my mom. My mom was on the receiving end of my verbal hostility during the first few days of the hospitalization. I actually told her on one occasion that I hated her and did not want her there with me. Although my doctor explained to her that this was part of the illness, it was hard for me to accept that I had hurt her; my mom has always been the most caring person and has shown me nothing but love.

I remained in Jefferson Hospital for twenty-eight days. By the time I left, the medications I took were lithium, Haldol, Trilafon, and Klonopin. (This is what I recall, but it is hard to remember.) By the end of my stay, I was really ready to leave and get back to school. The hospitalization process involved sending me home gradually with day trips to be sure I was ready to face the real world. For me this was the best way to do it, after being in such a safe haven; I wouldn't want to return abruptly. I began to do these home visits the last week of my stay. I was starting to get concerned about my schoolwork, and I still had difficulty concentrating, especially while reading. My teachers

13

had sent homework for my mom to bring to me in the hospital, but because of my concentration issues, I became very frustrated and was not able to accomplish much. My time-out was coming to an end.

I was discharged on March 29, 1984. Leaving the hospital was truly an emotional day, and I was not the only one crying. Although everyone was happy to see me leave (including my mom and myself), the patients and I were still going to miss one another. Twenty-eight days was a long period of time to bond with other people, and especially in such a unique situation, where I was with so many others who shared an illness with me. Also, in what part of most peoples' adult lives do they spend an entire month with someone else without going to school or work? I actually stayed in contact with a couple of the patients. I remember going with my mom, and then on my own, to visit another patient who had become a friend during our hospitalization. Although those who cared about me could sympathize and try to understand my illness, it was different with this friend. Continuing the friendship posthospitalization meant I had someone to talk to with a similar illness who understood what I was going through.

Once I was discharged, I could not wait to get back to school and see everyone. I had so much there waiting for me and wanted to get back to my normal life. My doctor warned me that people might talk about me behind my back and make remarks, but that did not worry me much at the time. Although it may have happened, I never knew or heard any such talk, which was a wonderful thing. While in the hospital both my parents and I made contact with my close friends and family. My diagnosis was not a secret or seen as something shameful; it was viewed just like any other illness that required hospitalization. It was a discussion of concern and compassion, not judgment. Not everyone fully comprehended what was going on, yet they attempted to gain some sort of understanding. Supporting me was more important than their need to fully understand.

I soon began to feel very different from others. One of my biggest frustrations in readjusting to school had to do with side effects from my medication. The lithium continued to cause me to have tremors, and my hands shook badly when trying to write. I was very aware of it, felt that others were noticing, and was embarrassed. I still had trouble concentrating, and that also made school difficult. I told my psychiatrist about these side effects at my first appointment, one week after leaving the hospital. As a result, he put me on the long-acting formulation of lithium, called Lithobid. Almost instantly the tremors went away. I remember my doctor frequently having me hold out my two hands to see if I had tremors. It was very disturbing; in order to be sure the lithium was not too high (toxic) or too low (ineffective), it was necessary to have my blood drawn and monitored to keep the amount of lithium in my system at a therapeutic level. At first I had my lithium levels checked very frequently, but over time it went from once a week to once a month to every other month, and now it is about twice a year. I continued to see my psychiatrist once a week, and then these visits also became less frequent as time passed.

As a consequence of this first hospitalization, I began to notice within myself that there now was one more difference that separated me from my friends: I was no longer on the same timeline in school. I went on to finish up my senior year, although I was a bit behind after having missed an entire month of classes. Actually, the time lost was more than two months, once I added in the days lost to the mania prior to my hospitalization, when I was not functioning at my full capacity. It was not easy being behind, but in time I did return to feeling quite normal day in and day out. As I think back now, I cannot believe how much strength I had to go back and face everyone. I honestly do not think I thought of it as having strength or anything positive about me; it was simply something I had to do.

I did not go to the prom, and that was very bothersome to me. Perhaps it was the first real rejection I felt that had to do with my illness. I was told by my friends that there was someone who wanted to ask me, but it was someone I was not interested in, and I told my friends I did not want to go with him. I guess that made me feel a little better, knowing someone was interested, but even so I basically felt like a loser. I thought that guys were afraid of me or thought I was strange because of what had happened. No one actually made me feel like I was strange; it was just my perception. Many people did not even know what had happened, let alone understand it. None of the students seemed to have heard of manic depression.

Although I was able to walk through graduation, I did not officially graduate. Even though many probably did not know I was not officially graduating, *I* knew and *I* cared—again I felt like I was different, and now it was because of my illness. I would officially graduate upon completion of my English research paper, which I had to do in the summer, and that part was awful. All my friends were out partying, celebrating the end of high school and the beginning of college, but I was worried about that damn paper. Nonetheless, I finished it and received my diploma one month late.

During the rest of the summer, I had what I would call a normal summer, spending time with friends and preparing for college. In September 1984, as planned, I went to Michigan State University (MSU) to pursue a degree in hotel and restaurant management. My mom was concerned that maybe I should not go so far away after what had happened, but my doctor thought it would be good to continue forward as planned; I should not be treated differently or treat my life differently because of this illness, and I should still be able to live a normal life.

When I left for MSU, the only medication I was on was lithium. I must say, I accepted my illness very quickly and did not question the validity of it. While in the hospital, my parents told me that my uncle was also manic-depressive. This helped with my acceptance, because we knew the illness was genetic. I was also very compliant with my medication; I would not dream of stopping my medication unless ordered by the doctor. I was not afraid of a manic episode happening again, although I knew it was possible. At age eighteen, I was not thinking that far into the future and worrying about what might be.

Chapter 3
Credit Cards, Rental Cars, and
Champagne Parties: Hospitalization #2

WHEN I STARTED AT Michigan State University in 1984, I was introduced to a new psychiatrist. Other than that and taking my lithium, I felt my life was quite normal. I also had the comfort that no one knew about my illness; it would be like getting a fresh start. I made many friends and became involved in the Student Alumni Association, where I gave prospective students and their families walking tours of the campus.

Freshman year took many interesting turns. In the fall I had an appendectomy just one month after I arrived at MSU. My mom immediately came to be with me. It was strange to have an emergency surgery while in a new environment. The appendectomy put me back a bit academically, but I did not go home and was able to stay at school and continue with the semester. I had made a few friends in a short time at this big school, and I had an old family friend who also attended MSU, which helped to make this difficult experience easier. The stress and pressure of a new environment, combined with a surgery that caused me to get behind in school, had no effect on my mental status or my medication. I am quite sure I never even considered the illness at this point (or the idea that this sort of thing could be a trigger). To me, this was something physical, and it was very separate from my mental illness.

For reasons that still do not make total sense to me, in January 1985 (my second trimester freshman year), my psychiatrist at MSU chose to take me off the lithium. While at MSU, I saw psychiatrists through the university's psychiatry department, and their care protocol was for each client to see a new psychiatrist each trimester. I had initially seen the head of psychiatry, but then I was switched to residents who rotated through. This particular resident I saw in January said my lithium levels were going down so low that they were not therapeutic, and therefore I did not need the lithium anymore. She slowly tapered me off until I was not taking any lithium at all.

Her reasoning for taking me off the medication made sense to me; however, I did not know at the time that some people get benefits from a nontherapeutic level, and apparently she must not have been aware of that, either. By taking me completely off my only medication, it seemed as if she was equating the lack of necessity for the lithium to the illness suddenly no longer existing. Why else would she discontinue the lithium and not add another medication, if I still had the illness? What would have made more sense was that she could have increased the dosage of my lithium until it got to a therapeutic level or because I was doing well, she could have continued me on the same dose. At the time, though, I felt great without the lithium and even lost fifteen pounds in a couple weeks without doing anything different. This certainly was my proof of the weight gain side effect of lithium for me.

Over a full year passed with no problems with the manic-depressive illness, and that was a huge blessing. Within that time period I did get mono in the spring semester, but again, although it set me back a bit academically, the stress of it had no effect on the illness (and I also had no meds on board). The more time went on without incident or worry, the less I thought about it. I thought perhaps the illness might never show up again.

However, just before Thanksgiving during my sophomore year, while on the phone with my mom, she recognized something similar to my first manic episode. I was talking fast and jumping from subject to subject. She sensed that something was not right. On her own, my mom spoke with my psychiatrist in Pittsburgh about my recent behavioral changes and he suggested she contact my psychiatrist at MSU to put me back on lithium. My psychiatrist at MSU concurred and prescribed lithium for me again. As happy as I was to be off medication, I really did not have a problem restarting it, mainly because I was following the doctor's orders. Adhering to my treatment plan continued not to be an issue for me. I was feeling pretty good at this point—maybe a little too good.

Prior to going home for Thanksgiving, a male classmate living in my dorm committed suicide in the basement of his fraternity house. No one had a clue why, and there was no note. Although I did not know him well, I knew three of his fraternity brothers very well. The suicide affected me in a very serious way. I was saddened, and it was difficult for me to understand how badly he was hurting that he saw suicide as his only way out. He was very attractive and seemed to have a lot going for him. He appeared to be very confident, but it goes to show that we often have no idea what is going on with someone when we judge them primarily by how they appear.

While at home for Thanksgiving break, I was still so affected by the suicide that I was overcome by the fear of death. I can remember taking a bath and needing to get out for fear of drowning. This fear was new and strange for me. I had been a lifeguard and swim instructor, and I also swam competitively for four years. I was not one to fear water, let alone a bathtub—yet I was scared to death of death and totally consumed with the thought of it. Although experiencing the aftereffects of a suicide was a lot for any student to deal with in a college setting, I feel my reaction was a bit over the top.

I had an appointment with my psychiatrist while in Pittsburgh, who told me I was okay to return to MSU, finish up the semester, and then come home for Christmas break. My mom still sensed things were not completely right and suggested that I not go back to MSU even just for those three weeks, but because the doctor said it was okay, my mom went along with his recommendation. My mania at this point was coming and going, and at the time I had not heard of the term *hypomania*, the milder form of mania. I realize now, in hindsight, that this is what I was experiencing, not full-blown mania. With hypomania, I now understand that I am better at controlling myself, and perhaps that was why the doctor perceived me as okay.

Upon my return to MSU, my judgment was not quite right. The first thing I was confronted with when I returned (and the first bit of real manic evidence) came when I received word that a friend of mine had been in a car accident. He and I had something together (a little more than a friendship, as he definitely showed his interest in me), but he also had a friend with whom he had an on-and-off relationship; he had told me they were not serious. Before I went home for Thanksgiving I told him it was only fair to me for us to be friends, and he agreed. For some reason, when I returned I had a feeling that something bad happened to him, and I called to check in and see if he was okay. His roommate said he had been in a bad car accident and was in the hospital in Dayton, Ohio. He and his "friend" were driving to his mom's in Florida. Perhaps she was more of a girlfriend than he had led me to believe. It was raining terribly that night, she was driving, they hydroplaned, and he did not have his seatbelt on and ended up injuring his back. He was very fortunate not to be paralyzed.

I *had* to go see him. What if he died? This really was not out of the ordinary behavior for me for a good friend—however we weren't that close, and the circumstance of where he was made a difference. It would have made a lot more sense for me to visit him in the hospital if it was local. Nevertheless, I had to see him, but how would I get to him?

I quickly proceeded to rent a car. As a college student with no job, I certainly did not have the extra money to do this, but when you are manic, you really don't think, you just act. In this case, I was thankful for the invention of credit cards. One of my friends offered to go along with me. In the meantime I also called a friend, John, whom I knew from high school and who coincidentally attended the University of Dayton. He said I could stay with him and his roommates. (Looking back, that was really amazing—I was not *that* close to him in high school. I now wonder just what he must have been thinking when I called him out of the blue. How I so quickly pulled his information out from my memory, I'm not really sure, but the brain is capable of much when you are in a manic state.) So then it was all set. This is when the judgment totally began to leave me, and oh boy, did I fall fast.

My friend drove most of the way because I was a wreck. John and his roommates welcomed us, and then the two of us were off to the hospital to see my injured friend. It was great seeing him, but something seemed to be up his sleeve. I started thinking there was some big plan for me in the making, and everything that was occurring seemed to be happening for a reason that revolved around me. I gave him my favorite Gund stuffed animal, a graduation gift from high school to take to college. I thought it would make him feel better and he could return it later. We left, and I told him I would come back the next day. On the way out we ran into his mother and sisters. Somehow I just knew and said, "Mrs. ———?" I knew we were connected instantly, and she said how wonderful it was that I came all that way for her son.

When we got back to John's, my friend from MSU decided that she wanted to go back that night. I was not ready to leave and told her to just drive the rental car back, and I would rent another one. Here I went again with the lack of judgment. If I did not have the money to rent the first car, how would I have it for the second? I hardly slept that night.

In the morning I began typing Mark's paper, at his request. Mark was John's roommate and was also from our high school, but someone I did not know well. I typed incredibly fast; my fingers flew across the keys of the typewriter, and yet somehow, it was accurate. Then John dropped me off at the hospital, and I visited with my friend and his sister. I still thought they were planning something for me. I left and said I would return one last time to say good-bye that night, because I would be returning to MSU in the morning.

I don't even know how I found the car rental place. I was walking downtown in an unfamiliar city in a confused fog. Because they were out of compact cars, they upgraded me to an Oldsmobile Cutlass Sierra. This was 1985 and I was young, so I really thought this was a great car and the upgrade was just for me. It was brand-new and also a Limited Selection model. Those were my initials, and I thought somehow the car was going to be mine. Everything was connected, and it all made total sense to me.

I drove back to John's, and the guys suggested I take a nap. I rarely listened to close friends or family while in a manic state and would often get defensive when they told me what to do. I think I was more inclined to listen to John and his friends because they were on the outskirts of my circle of friends and were not intimately involved in my life. I slept for several hours (which is hard for even me to conceive, because while in a manic episode sleeping was not something easy to do). Upon waking up, I did feel better, and the sense of confusion was gone. That evening I went back to the hospital, and my friend's mom said he was having a tough time adjusting to the medications and was very agitated; it was not a good time for me to see him. She seemed scared and we cried together. Who knows what any of them were thinking of me, but I never really thought about it at that time. I was in my own little world and loved life just as it was.

The next morning I got up around 5:00 a.m. to drive back in my new "LS" to MSU, not even slightly concerned about the other car and whether it had been returned. My judgment was as good as gone. I sped and smoked the entire way back to school. I would have a few cigarettes occasionally in a social setting, but smoking constantly, and in a car for that matter, was not my typical behavior. I eventually got a speeding ticket in Jackson, Michigan, which probably saved my life. I could have cared less about the ticket—why would I? I was high again and life was good. Nothing would get me down. I decided to find the Jackson City Hall to pay the ticket. I remember being very disoriented as to where I was going. I have no idea what made me go there to appear in person to pay the ticket when it had just occurred only minutes prior.

Reckless behavior is characteristic of a manic state. I didn't care about anything, was on top of the world, and was going nonstop. This may give a better understanding of why people do not want to take their medications when they are manic: it truly is giving up something that most people are not privileged (or cursed) to experience. Only in hindsight did I begin to understand the chemical and emotional pattern for me: as stressful or bad things came my way, my mood state would go up instead of down. This reversal easily sums up how my chemical imbalance affected me at that point.

I got back to MSU and kept the rental car for a few more days, enjoying the freedom to go where I wanted to with ease. After several more days of my manic behavior, a concerned friend of mine called my parents to apprise them of the changes in my demeanor. This friend did not know I was manic-depressive; she was simply worried about the way I was acting. My parents made the trip to MSU the next day to try to assess the situation and help me however they could. This same friend said to me, "Don't get upset, but your parents are coming."

My response? "I know." How I knew this or had a feeling this was true, I have no idea.

Because I still had the rental car, knowing they were coming the next day, I went shopping at a large chain discount store and bought them some clothes. I remember thinking I was getting all these great buys and put it all on my credit card, thinking nothing of it. My lack of judgment continued.

My parents arrived the next day, and I was happy to see them … at first. They took care of returning the car and made life a bit easier for me. I showed them the clothes I had purchased for them, and they immediately saw they were all the wrong sizes. As we held some of the items up to my mom, they were *huge,* and we were able to see the humor in it and laugh. (Although it was sad to think that the day before, I had no idea the sizes were not correct.) My parents took me back to the store, and we returned the clothes. For some parts of the day, the mania seemed to subside. At times I was actually behaving more like my regular self and appeared to be okay for a while. Perhaps being with my parents, along with them coming to my rescue by taking care of some of the problems I had created, offered a form of comfort, which helped to clear my thoughts.

As my mom and dad observed my behavior throughout the day, they realized that although I was not acting outrageously, I was definitely not myself, and they recognized the familiarity of my first manic episode. Taking full note of my behavior, my parents arranged for me to have an appointment at a nearby hospital, Ingham Medical Center in Lansing, Michigan, the very next day. I met with a psychologist and also another resident psychiatrist from the MSU psychiatry department—a female psychiatrist at that. I was not able to trust female psychiatrists or psychologists at this time, because it was a female psychiatrist who took me off the lithium at MSU. I was not pleased to meet with her. She and the psychologist conducted a short consultation. I told them I was upset with my parents, and I wanted them to leave. I somehow was able to slow down my thoughts and speech, act normal, and convince the doctors that I was okay enough to remain in school and that my parents should go back home. I felt I was able to control the behavior I was exhibiting, so I thought I was fine. I was not being very nice to my parents by telling them to leave. I feel this was the extent of the mean and irritable side of the illness that was showing up. (Although it is common during a manic episode, it rarely shows up for me.) Much to my parents' surprise, the female psychiatrist sent them home. My parents were concerned to leave me by myself. After the consultation, I was sent back to class without any changes in my medications.

My parents had great faith in doctors and did not go against what the psychiatrist thought was best for me. They left reluctantly and, deep down, felt this was not the right thing for me. In hindsight it upsets me deeply to know how traumatic it must have been for them to leave me.

Within a week, however, *I* felt something was not right and approached my original psychiatrist at MSU regarding my continued confusion and difficulties. He did not prescribe any medication changes, but he handled the paperwork for me to take the rest of the semester off and return after Christmas break. I complied and took incompletes for all my classes. While home, I didn't rest, but I worked at the Gap and went to a lot of Christmas parties, including my own open house.

After the holidays I returned to MSU in January 1986, where I had to start off the new semester with a full load of new classes and four incompletes—just a *little* bit stressful to add to my already fragile state. The ride back to school was interesting. My mom drove three of us from the area back to MSU, and I took just about everything but the kitchen sink.

Upon returning to school, I felt that something was not right again; I began to get confused and felt surreal in my environment. My recollection at this time is somewhat fragmented. In continuing treatment, I saw the same resident psychiatrist from Ingham Medical Center (the same one who had told my parents to go home). Given my current state, she prescribed Haldol to help clear up my thoughts. I remembered I had been on it while hospitalized in 1984.

While waiting for the Haldol to take effect, I experienced some terrifying moments. First I was walking and running aimlessly all over campus like a zombie, thoroughly disoriented and trying to get to my psychiatrist's office for a follow-up appointment. I could not focus enough to find the right campus bus and was late, therefore missing that appointment. The doctor and the staff were not too happy with me. They did, however, reschedule me for later that day with a different psychiatrist at the opposite end of campus, with which I was not familiar. I cannot understand how they thought I could have made it safely, or at all, to find this second psychiatrist appointment location in the state I was in—unless they truly could not see through my behavior and responses that I was very ill.

I ended up going on foot to this next appointment. I ran through heavily falling snow a good thirty minutes in order to make it there. I was in a completely frustrated and bewildered state. When I actually saw the psychiatrist, he did very little except to make sure I was on my medication, which meant continuing with the lithium and Haldol. I had requested this psychiatry appointment asking for medication or another type of intervention. To my astonishment, he thought I was okay enough and sent me back to my dorm to rest and then go back to continue with my coursework. He was well aware that I had just returned to begin my five-course load along with the four incompletes from the first semester—pretty stressful, to say the least. I was basically alone, confused, and very misunderstood by the doctors. Per his instructions, I went back to my dorm. I would be attempting to get back to my academic routine in the midst of a manic episode that was not recognized as such.

I later felt that these doctors must have not dealt with many manic-depressive patients, otherwise they may have tried to help me more. Unlike the month prior, when I wanted my parents sent home because I thought I was fine and had control of my behavior, this time *I* knew something was wrong, and *I* was asking for help, but people treated me as if I was fine.

By early that evening my muscles were so stiff that I could barely move. My speech was slurred, and it sounded as if I were drunk. I also began drooling for no apparent reason. My thoughts were okay, and I clearly knew what was physically occurring but was unable to control it or stop it from worsening. It was very scary. Soon I could hardly move my jaw to speak. All of this was going on in my dorm for others to witness. I still cannot get over that so many people had to see me like this.

Thank goodness for my friend Don, who lived in my dorm. He and two other friends took me to the emergency room, having to help me into the car. By this point, we were all frightened. When in the ER, they immediately gave me an injection of Cogentin. Within five minutes I was totally back to normal, at least physically. The ER doctor then prescribed me Cogentin in the pill form and told me that this was all that the female psychiatrist had to do from the beginning to prevent all the scariness, pain, and embarrassment. Forgetting that one major detail—to prescribe the Cogentin to counteract the stiffness induced by the Haldol—was huge. Of course, I felt I was not given the best treatment.

The emotional scarring from this episode lasted a very long time and was not good for my well-being. The worst part of it all was that it took place in my college dorm for others to hear, see, know, and talk about. I was concerned about what they would think of me. Similar to my high school setting, very few people in that dorm, if any, understood what was going on. A meeting took place where the resident assistant tried to help others on my floor to understand what was happening to me, but I do not know what was discussed, where she got her information from, or what her level of understanding of the illness was.

After the whole experience with the ER as a result of the medication errors, and after what had happened earlier that same day with my attempts to get to the psychiatrist's office, I felt I could not do it on my own and should be hospitalized. I wanted so badly for the doctors to acknowledge my distress, but the psychiatrist kept telling me I was okay. So, without any additional medical intervention, the mania continued on its course.

Shortly after the trip to the ER, I planned and organized a champagne party in my dorm room. I met a guy from MSU who happened to be in the champagne business, and he was able to get me a couple of cases of champagne for a good deal. (Where was the money going to come from, and who had champagne parties in their dorm rooms? This part of the illness is very hard to understand. Once the judgment goes, it goes in lots of areas. Somehow, whatever is going on in the brain causes many who experience mania to have no concept of money. You just spend and spend as if it grows on trees.)

The confusion and mania came and went. Sometimes I seemed to be okay, and probably to some people, I really was. But after two months of this, I was at the point where I could not take it anymore. I knew something was wrong. After several additional attempts of asking for help, I was finally able to get my point across to the head psychiatrist at MSU. He spoke with that same female psychiatrist from the Ingham Medical Center in Lansing and requested that I go there to be evaluated. I now had some hope, and yes, I was still sort of high.

I had much difficulty figuring out the public bus transportation system to get to Lansing. I was in such a clouded state of mind and could not process much information on my own. I called my father, and he called our family friend Tim, also a student at MSU, to ask if he would call me to ensure I got on the right bus. Without his help, I could have ended up just about anywhere.

Once on the bus, I began to feel my first sense of relief; hospitals meant safety to me. The thirty-minute ride was one I still remember. I went straight toward the back of the bus, sat with about six male African American kids, and started rapping with them. No, I was not your typical white rapper girl, but it just seemed to be what was supposed to happen. The mania seems to tap into a more creative side and connects everything, and I would go where it took me. The kids on the bus were so nice to me. Who knows if they thought this was normal for me—I did not care, and we had a lot of fun.

Once I got to the hospital, two psychiatrists evaluated me—one being that same dreadful woman who prescribed the Haldol without the Cogentin. Why did I have to see her again after what she did to me previously? This time, with the help of the other doctor, I was able to show her that, indeed, I was not fine. She now realized I really had needed some additional help. You think? After I broke down crying, they both agreed I needed to be hospitalized. It certainly took too long to come to this decision. So much could have been avoided had they recognized my behavior as manic the first time I had an appointment back in December. I wish they could have trusted my parents' judgment over mine. (Now, I have a different insight and wonder if, because I was over the age of eighteen and they did not feel I was in danger of hurting myself or others, perhaps their hands were tied. This explanation was not ever conveyed to my parents or me.)

When it came to hospitalization, my behavior was contradictory to some in that many people did everything they could to avoid the hospital, and I was doing everything I could do get *into* the hospital. My cry for help was not successful until much later. Today it troubles me to think about the way things were handled, but this was over twenty years ago, and with more information and the advancements in medicine, I like to believe we are now able to recognize signs and symptoms more readily. I am glad that my perseverance eventually paid off and that I was able to get the proper care I needed.

I was immediately admitted to Ingham Medical Center. I felt the care I received there was very good. The psychiatric area was very small compared with where I had been before. There were only six rooms, and I had a roommate, which was different from my prior hospitalization. The staff certainly made me feel special there, and that was very helpful to my recovery. The first night I could not believe that they served me steak in bed. I felt like a princess! This hospital stay was a short ten days, but it was tough because this time I was away from home and felt very lonely. Additionally, I was beginning to understand my illness and recognized that I needed help to the point where I had to be my own advocate and initiate treatment, as opposed to the first time when I was told what to do.

My roommate was from the local area and had six family visitors my first night. The overwhelming support she received did the opposite for me: I remember crying because I so desired the attention she was receiving, which was what I had received during my first hospitalization. I knew that I, too, had many people who supported me; they just weren't there because I was so far away from home. In a way, this was an abrupt way of beginning to bring me back to reality. I believe the mania was beginning to make a bit of a shift, not actually to depression, but because I had been so high, just getting closer to normal was an extreme transition.

After a few days at Ingham Medical Center, my mother and a family friend came to visit me and stayed for about a week. Now my support system was back, and it really made a difference.

Although having a roommate was initially difficult, in the end it proved to be beneficial. She was so nice and also made me laugh. It's funny how a person so severely depressed could make me laugh. We were positive support for each other. She would tell people, "She's manic and I'm depressed, and together we make the manic-depressive illness." I liked the way she put it, because overall I really did not feel depressed. It was rough, being treated for too much happiness; obviously there was a lot more to this illness than feeling high, but that was how it sometimes felt to me. We both learned a lot about each other's illnesses, increasing our awareness and understanding of affective mood disorders. Our relationship played a role in both of our recoveries.

Dr. K. was my psychiatrist while at Ingham, and I thought he was a great psychiatrist. He got right to the point, changed up my medications, and had me discharged quickly. That I liked. Dr. K. wanted me to return to reality as soon as possible. His opinion was that the faster I returned to my normal routine, the better; lengthy hospital stays would only prolong my recovery. My father was very impressed compared with the amount of time I had previously spent in the hospital, but this time we were ahead of the curve because I already had the diagnosis and meds on board.

Upon discharge, I returned home to Pittsburgh instead of MSU to begin my recovery again. I was trying to gain an understanding of the reality of all that had occurred during this manic episode. My parents let me know that in addition to everything else, I had also bounced many checks. I had no recollection of this. Apparently, I was spending money freely and had no idea there were no funds in my account to cover the checks. This is when it really hit home to me just how sick I truly was.

Mom and I took a trip to Florida to see my grandparents and to take a break from all the stress and pressure I had endured over the past four months.

After my time-out in Florida, and with a clearer head, I decided I wanted to return to MSU after spring break in time for the beginning of the third trimester. This time my dad took me. We moved everything to a new room; I had a single in the same dorm I was in before. Within only a few days, I decided I was not ready. Something just did not feel right to me. I don't really know exactly what went on, except that I really did not feel comfortable. I guess I was a little scared and probably not totally up to the academics. I think facing everyone would have been very tough, but I'm not sure if that was what I was thinking at the time; it was more of an overwhelming feeling. My dad had to come back, we packed everything up again, and I moved back home.

For the remaining months until it was time for school to start again in the fall, I worked and enjoyed the summer. Things became normal over time, and I was able to handle life again. I enrolled in the class Introduction to Sociology at the University of Pittsburgh so I could feel as if I was being productive. It was interesting, because the class had nothing to do with my current major, and years later that was the major with which I graduated. After working as a cook at a pizza place for the majority of the summer (which was the worst job ever), I went on a three-week vacation to Hilton Head, South Carolina, with my best friend from MSU. We had a blast. When I returned home, the summer was basically over, and it was time to move ahead with the next phase of my life.

I now had a difficult decision to make. After all that had happened, would I really return to MSU as planned? I had already attempted to return a couple times, only to end up back home. So many people had told me it was okay not to go back, or maybe perhaps even better, because the potential of having to face people who saw me act the way I did could be intimidating. Questions by those who cared were put to me about whether or not I should allow myself to go through with it all over again, reliving those awful times just by being back there. However, I thought exactly the opposite on this one. I felt that facing everything would be very courageous and empowering, and it was probably something that many would not do. I had a strong desire to go back, and if I chose to leave MSU, I did not want it to be because of my illness. I felt that staying home would be like running away from my fears.

I returned to MSU in the fall of 1986. I stayed in the same complex of dorms, but around the corner from my previous dorm. I had a new roommate, and we got along just fine. I met a really nice new group of girls on my floor, and we became friends very quickly. No one judged me, and they had no idea what had gone on the previous year (unless I decided to share some of it). Part of this probably had to do with the size of MSU: at the time there were forty-eight thousand students there. I did let my new roommate know about my illness because she was my roommate. There was no apparent judgment made on her end, and no issues developed as a result of me having bipolar disorder.

My third year at MSU (but second academically due to the lapse) proved to be very good, both physically and emotionally. My best friend was still there but living off campus, and I still saw her quite often. The year back proved to be a lot of fun overall, but I realized I did not know what I wanted to do academically; I had switched my major from hotel and restaurant management to communications. I felt it was not fair to my parents to continue to pay for my education when I was unsure which major to pursue (and considering I was having so much fun). After the year was up, I decided to move back home. Now it was my decision (and not because of the illness), and I was thrilled that I gave MSU and myself another chance. Going back was clearly not only the right decision for me, but probably one of the best decisions I have ever made. I learned for myself what kind of strength I really had and how I had grown so quickly, both in my character and in my emotional well-being.

I believe the onset of my second manic episode began with me doing too many things at once, and the role that sleep played was definitely a factor. I'm not clear on whether it was induced sleep deprivation that came first and helped to trigger the mania, or if the mania caused the lack of sleep and then the cycle continued. Either way, the sleep deficiency clearly made things worse. This particular episode was really rough and continued with several months of mania, both in mild and extreme forms.

Throughout this manic episode, once again, my parents were a great support, but this time there was a new symptom: overspending. Without my parents' help with the financial expenditures that were a result of my grandiose ideas, I would have been in real trouble. Fortunately for me, however, the financial damage was not too terrible: my expenses came to somewhere between one and two thousand dollars. This was a substantial amount for a college student to cover, and I was fortunate to have parents who were willing to bail me out because they knew I was not spending intentionally. I have heard numerous stories of people losing anywhere from many thousands up to millions of dollars and losing careers, dreams, or life savings from mania-induced spending sprees.

Following my second manic episode, the continuing cycle of uphill challenges began. It was incredibly difficult each time, starting over and picking up the pieces from where I had left off, knowing all I had done during my manic phases. I felt like my self-esteem had been taken, like a rug being pulled out from under me. I had to start again at zero and build myself up. Although I was not so concerned about what others thought during my manic episodes, I did have to face everything and everyone once it was over. This was a tall order.

The second mania (and how it presented itself in both hypomania and full-blown mania) and the hospitalization were the beginning of my awareness of what bipolar would mean in my life and how to maintain what normal looked like to me. I was trying very hard not to let the illness take away the normalcy from my life. I was a college student in my early twenties, trying to feel my way through as anyone at this age would be doing—never mind doing it with bipolar disorder and always knowing it was there.

Chapter 4
My Little Corner of Hell: Hospitalization #3

IN JUNE OF 1987, after completing two years and one trimester at Michigan State University and realizing I was unclear about my major course of study, I moved back in with my parents and continued my education close to home. It had only been three years since this illness found me, and it certainly consumed a lot of those three years. So much had changed so quickly, which skewed how I had envisioned this time in my life would look. Leaving the environment of full-time university study meant I would not be keeping in line with my peers. Living with my parents instead of the dorms or off-campus housing would be different, too.

I enrolled part-time at the University of Pittsburgh in the fall of 1987 and also worked about twenty-five hours a week at the university's health center. I was able to sustain a more structured environment that ensured moving forward with my educational goals. My health had stabilized, and I experienced another full year (actually nineteen months) without any major incident. Life had returned to normal in many ways, and I enjoyed the steady and stabilized routine and socializing with friends.

In the summer of 1988, I enrolled full-time at Pitt and worked part-time as a student employee in the dean's office for graduate studies. I worked with some really great people and enjoyed the job between classes. My high school friend Andrea had transferred to

Pitt and was living at home, too. She introduced me to one of her new college friends, and the three of us hung out together a lot.

The gradual progression of my third manic episode began at the tail end of August 1988 and continued for several months, ultimately resulting in my third hospitalization that November. Throughout this episode I was back on the lithium; however, because I had been taken off it the year prior, the lithium alone was not enough to hold me through the series of situational triggers that were about to occur. For some, when lithium is reintroduced, it is not as efficacious as when first prescribed, and additional medications are necessary to achieve the same effect. Perhaps this third mania would not have escalated had I not been taken off the lithium several years prior.

My thought is that this onset of mania began during a brief vacation to Rehoboth Beach, Delaware, just before the start of Labor Day weekend with my good friend Diane. For a couple nights in a row, we were out late and had quite a bit to drink. The second night at the beach I met a guy with whom I was so impressed because he was a pitcher for the University of North Carolina baseball team—*and* he was interested in me. We flirted and hung out for a few hours late into the night. This was not typical behavior for me because I had a boyfriend back home whom I had been dating for a couple months that summer.

Whether my behavior was due to the alcohol alone, or whether the mania contributed to the excess consumption (or if it was a combination of the two influencing the other), I am unclear. What is clear to me is that my boyfriend's feelings did not come into play for me that night. In fact, it was like he did not even exist. My lack of judgment and consideration for him indicates to me that the mania was part of the equation, because I know I would not have done this no matter how much alcohol I consumed. I am as loyal as they come in regard to my relationships.

The role of sleep deprivation contributing to the mania is also unclear. My sleep patterns were off, and the smallest of changes, even for a short duration of time, may have had an effect, pushing me toward the mania when everything else was lining up.

Upon returning from our trip, I felt very good about myself. Up until the vacation, the relationship I had with my boyfriend seemed to be going just fine. However, two days after returning home, I gave my boyfriend his birthday present, which I bought while on vacation, and I broke up with him at the same moment. I don't remember feeling all that bad about it; I was moving on to bigger and better things, because I could. I have no idea if he understood the mixed message of the simultaneous gift giving and breakup. I did not even understand it myself at that time.

Shortly after that long weekend, as I was continuing to feel good about myself, Andrea and her friend took me to a party, introducing me to a male friend of the two guys they were sort of dating. He and I hit it off instantly. The six of us left the party and decided to go over to one of the guy's parents' home, in a suburb of Pittsburgh. The complex they lived in had a pool, and he wanted to go swimming. We had brought our suits because the party we had been at had a hot tub (although we never went in). The other four decided it was too cold to swim, but I was game—I love swimming and thought it would be fun. We had to jump over a locked fence, which was not a big deal to me (and made it more of an adventure). I put my suit on and was ready to go.

We had both consumed alcohol, but I never finished my second beer, so I don't consider it to be a factor in my behavior. While in the pool, he kissed me and then wanted to take it further. I did not. We got out of the pool, and I sat on one of the lounge chairs. He got on top of me and tried his darndest to move my suit out of the way to have sex. I told him no at least ten times, and I was shaken by his insistence. What started as an adventure had taken a terrifying turn. He kept badgering me, saying things like, "What's wrong with you? Haven't you ever had good sex before?" I was so scared and felt powerless and weak, so I finally gave in. I could not fight back anymore. I remember just lying there. I did not move. I just let him take over me. After it happened, I felt nothing emotionally, and physically I felt numb.

For a long time, I put the responsibility on myself for the so-called date rape. I actually did not even see it as rape—I blamed myself for this guy forcing himself on me, even when the choice did not appear to be mine. I saw it as my fault for being spontaneous and having fun and allowing myself to be alone with him. Even though it was not logical, I saw myself as an equal participant.

35

I suppressed any notions that he had raped me, to the extent that I went to see him shortly after the pool incident, when a friend of his had passed away. I wanted to be there to comfort him. How I could want to do this, after knowing he had forced himself on me, I really can't explain. My thinking was warped, and I know that the fact he wanted to see me again and showed a real interest in me was more important. I liked him. He called to go out while he was still in Pittsburgh, which did not work out because of his job. He then wrote me a letter right away when he returned to Boston for college, and he expressed an interest for me to visit him and for us to date. I, too, wanted our relationship to continue.

In the midst of all that was going on, I moved on October 1, 1988, into a little apartment in Mt. Lebanon, which was about five miles from where my parents lived. I now think what initiated the move was the result of the phases of the manic episode showing up. Prior to the move, I was going out all the time (which was typical for me), and my mom was always worried about me, waiting up for me. I kept saying I was twenty-two years old and responsible. I was fine. She did not need to worry or wait up. I only know now that she *did* have reason to worry about me—not because of my late nights, but because the mania had begun to come about again. During manic phases my usual behavior is somewhat heightened. As I have said before, I feel that the manias are extensions of me, although sometimes they are extreme.

As a result of what was already a very traumatic incident (even though I was not really seeing it that way), I found out I was pregnant. This came as a shock and brought much fear to me, especially because of what I had been told about the medications I was on. My ob-gyn told me that an abortion was my only option because of the birth defects that were highly likely with lithium: teratogenic abnormalities (embryonic development), particularly congenital heart defects known as Ebstein's anomaly. (However, more recent data substantiates a reduction for the risk estimates of Ebstein's anomaly from a range of 1 in 1,000 to 1 in 20,000 live births.)[1] Although I was not prepared to have a baby, the thought of having an abortion sickened me. In fact, it nearly killed me emotionally. I could not come to terms that I would actually be taking a life. I endured an enormous amount of pain and guilt. Further, it was something else I felt over which I did not have a whole lot of choice. I pretty much did what I was told by my doctor, and I could not think much further than that. The mania was continuing to come and go, but I know my lack of sleep was making it worse. My lack of sleep was caused by the mania rather than being self-induced at this point.

I felt I had to call the would-be father right away to let him know about the pregnancy and the need for an abortion. When I called him with this news, I think he felt a little bad, but there was not a whole lot of comfort or compassion there. In order to try to make him feel *something* and to take some responsibility for what had occurred, I told him I was going to have to pay for the procedure out of pocket and expected him to pay for half of it. I lied to him knowingly, because I knew my insurance was going to cover the full expense. He mailed a check, and I ripped it up immediately because I had intended to teach him a lesson, not to take his money. It was a big enough deal that I led him to believe he had to pay for it at all, and I felt I needed to be honest with him in the end. As planned, I later told him the truth.

In addition to suppressing the date rape, discovering I was pregnant, and realizing an abortion was the only option—compounded with the dismissal by the would-be father—I was extremely overwhelmed and was kind of in a fog. I was trying to take it all in, but a true sense of logic was lost along the way. For a little while I was too exhausted to think anymore. During this time, beginning after the date rape incident, I was clinging to anyone I felt close to, including a couple of my guy friends. Each tried to offer me comfort but did not really understand what was going on because I did not tell them what had happened. They comforted me in ways they could, but there was not much emotional support for them to lend; it was more of physical support—just to be held closely was what I seemed to need. Perhaps I was replacing the comfort and closeness I was missing from the would-be father with others I knew and felt safe with. My ability to react and respond to the compounding traumatic events became more difficult. The mania was definitely present, but I believe it was fluctuating between hypomania and full-blown mania.

On a Tuesday morning in early October, I took the trolley downtown to the clinic. Outside there were pro-lifers picketing and yelling things, and I tried to ignore them. They did not know my situation, and screaming rude things certainly was not going to help matters or make me change my mind.

The whole experience was quite horrific. I can remember lying there on the table. Once the procedure began, I felt as if the life was being sucked out of me—literally and figuratively. I could have never imagined how awful it was going to be in that traumatizing moment. I was already having such a difficult time with the necessity of what I had to do, but when it ultimately occurred, I could not have imagined anything worse. Two of my friends met me afterward, took me to lunch although I was feeling quite sick, and then brought me home. I was emotionally detached, but I appreciated their intention to be with me in this moment of grief so that I would not be alone.

I knew I was in need of being with friends, so a few days later I drove to MSU for homecoming, to spend time with some close friends. How I could have driven six hours so soon after that procedure is extremely difficult for me to comprehend, but it is something that can only be explained by the illness. And with my judgment on a temporary hiatus, it was easier to understand.

While I was visiting my friends at MSU, I had to go to the emergency room because I couldn't stop bleeding. I was very scared, as were my friends; I had told them about the abortion. The ER doctor gave me something to stop the bleeding. I had thought all along the abortion was done too early, but my ob-gyn disregarded the dates I had recorded. I ended up bleeding for another four weeks, but not nearly as badly as it was initially. I did not let the excessive bleeding get me down and had a great weekend. I drove back to my apartment on Sunday and somehow made it back safely. My brother, who was home on break from college, surprised me that night with a visit with two of his friends. He was sure something was not quite right with me, but he did not know what to do.

Three weeks later I was headed to Boston. I felt I needed to see this person I had created this baby with, to gain some comfort and understanding. The trip, however, did not go too well. From the very start there were issues. After getting off the plane in Boston, I was

38

paged over the intercom to pick up a courtesy phone. He was on the other end and had been in a car accident on the way to pick me up. He was okay, but he needed to let me know he would not be picking me up and instructed me to take a cab to his apartment. I felt this was a sign of what was to come. Fortunately for me, I had a friend from MSU living in Boston, and I had already made arrangements to see her as well.

The next two days were sheer hell with him. We argued until we could not speak anymore. He told me I had no good qualities and was a very bad person. He thought I was making too big of a deal of the whole pregnancy and abortion, and he thought I should get over it immediately. He was really quite mean and hurtful. Through all my painful emotions, I could not see through him to realize his reactions were not about me, but more about him. Later that evening, after the dust had begun to settle, he shared with me some depression problems of his own—and his suicide attempt the previous year. Although I realized the two of us were not any help to each other, I still felt some sort of bond with him. However, that bond was fading fast. I really did not know what to do at that moment, so I called my friend from MSU to come pick me up earlier than planned. She came to my rescue.

My friend helped me to regain positive thoughts of myself and tune out all that this guy had branded in my brain. She was a true angel and totally took care of me, as I thought he would have done. I was still coming in and out of this manic state, not sleeping so well, and all the signs and connections continued to be there as they had been in previous manic episodes. I went shopping in the area around Boston University and found myself in a used bookstore. Each book I picked up had inner meaning, and things were connecting to one another again. I came home with a whole bunch of these used books and then signed my name on the inside cover of each one. I still have them to this day and have tried to figure out just what the inner meaning of it all was and how everything connected.

Upon returning to my apartment in Mt. Lebanon, and with the feelings I thought I was going to find in Boston not fulfilled, I was emotionally lost. At the same time my mania was coming and going. I continued not to be able to sleep. During this manic episode it was truly fascinating to see and experience my ability to draw. I have always had the desire to draw, but it is simply not a gift I possess, with the exception of this manic episode. It is still amazing to me how complicated our brains are—does that mean this creative side of me really exists somewhere? I also felt that spiritual closeness with God again, and although I was totally distraught because of the loss, that aspect did help some. However, my thoughts were racing; I could not shut my brain off, and I was going from one activity to another (including trying to organize anything I could find). I could not focus on any one thing for too long.

I decided to tell my family about all that had been going on. I just could not handle it all on my own anymore. My brother said to me, "Lizabeth, if you can't tell your family, who loves and cares about you so much, then who can you really tell?" He was right; however, I cannot believe I shared it with them and with many others. Although by nature I am a very open person, sharing uninhibitedly without worry was due to the mania.

Upon hearing the news, my father was outraged and wanted to tear this guy apart. I immediately defended him and said it was just as much my responsibility as his. (I now realize I must have done this either because I knew I had bigger things to worry about, or because I still felt some sort of bond with him. I'm not totally clear on that.) My biggest and more difficult issue was how I was now going to deal with what I had done: actually taken the life of this unborn child, *my* child. I certainly feared my family's reaction to my situation, but again I was reminded of just how fortunate I was. Their reaction was the opposite of what I had expected: they offered all the love and support possible. They could see the severe pain I was in, and their comfort meant so much to me.

Two days later was election day, and I was working for NBC doing exit-poll reporting up in the North Hills section of Pittsburgh. I remember getting completely lost. I stopped at least five times to ask for directions, and I could not find the voting venue. I felt as if I were in a fog, a feeling that was not unfamiliar to me. I somehow managed to find it and completed the job. I was okay, but not for long. I had to call in all the results, and I called them into a man in Philadelphia. He and I totally connected on the phone and later talked again. He had been paralyzed from injuring his spine while diving into a wave in the ocean, and in an instant, life as he knew it would never be the same. I do not know to this day if our connection was due entirely to the mania or not. He was actually going to come visit me, but that never panned out. I certainly have been known to connect with people instantly, but normally it was not on the phone with a complete stranger.

Immediately following the exit polling that night, I was off! I drove about seventy miles to another state for a Young Republicans party at the home of some friends. I sped the entire way with a cigarette in one hand and a beer in the other. As mentioned before, I was not a smoker and certainly had never drunk alcohol while driving. This was incredibly reckless, manic behavior. The party went well, and after it ended my friend and I went to various bars and continued our drinking. We had a lot of fun.

I spent the night and woke up to the shocking news of the death of my friend's mom. Her father had recently passed away as well, and now she was hit with the realization that both her parents were gone. Because her husband was out of town, I took it upon myself to make her feel better. We picked up her daughter from school, and then I drove them the hour and thirty minutes back to Pittsburgh to stay at my place. My friend slept and I did not—I was a wreck. My mom was so worried about me by this time that she asked my younger sister, Susanne, to drive all three of us back to my friend's home, where I was to stay in, get rest, and come home early in the morning so that my sister could drive back to be at school by 7:30 a.m. (she was seventeen and in high school).

Instead of going to bed and getting a good night's rest, my friend and I went out for a wild evening on the town. We made it back to my friend's house in time for a couple hours of sleep. As planned, Susanne drove me home the next morning. While in the car, I turned to her and asked her if she honestly thought I needed to go into the hospital. She said yes, and I think we both had tears in our eyes. Hearing her say that word and the look of fear in her eyes enabled me to come to the realization that something must be wrong.

That day I called my psychiatrist. I cannot remember exactly how it came to this, but I really wanted to go into the hospital and was sure I needed it. Initially my psychiatrist was against it, but I don't think she could detect on the phone the severity of my actions, and obviously she had not been around me the past few days. This seems to be a common occurrence for me: for some reason or other, I must appear better than I am, even to the professionals. I understand the importance of keeping people out of the hospital, but when the warning signs are clearly present and the patient is insisting the need for hospitalization, I just don't understand trying to dissuade the person. Through our conversation, I finally convinced my psychiatrist that hospitalization was something I needed. Persistence is a good thing at times. This is how hospitalization number three began.

I was admitted to St. Francis Hospital in Pittsburgh on November 10, 1988. All of this craziness needed to end, and I needed to regain control of my life. At intake, I went through the familiar process of being virtually strip-searched and feeling like I was being interrogated. Again, it was a pretty uncomfortable feeling. I was initially discharged eleven days later, but I could not regain the control I had hoped for and went back after a few days at home.

When I returned to the hospital for the second two weeks, I realized I would be stuck in the psych ward over Thanksgiving, which was not a lot of fun. I recall my family coming in shifts to visit me and bringing me turkey and all the fixings to try to make the holiday a little enjoyable. Having family there was definitely helpful. It was my brother's first visit to a psych unit, and I still remember the look in his eyes that made me realize he was quite uncomfortable. I recall a conversation we had later where he told me he had not been afraid of me, he just did not know what to expect from anyone else there. I realize this can be a frightening experience for those who care about us.

During this next part of my hospitalization, strange and new behaviors began to present themselves. I know I was having more side effects from the Haldol and other medications, but for some reason I got this idea in my head that I wanted to hurt myself physically. Part of me believes it was to gain attention, because I certainly did not really want to injure myself or to end my life. I remember scheming as to what I could use. Obviously, we were not permitted to have sharp objects. I remembered I had a fountain pen. I took it apart, getting black ink all over me in the process, and then I used the sharp end to cut my arm. I don't really know what possessed me to do this—it was the most bizarre behavior for me, and I was not thinking clearly. The hospital staff was not very concerned by my actions, and I guess that defeated my whole purpose.

I also remember getting irritable, causing some type of scene in the hall outside the nurses' station, and having a physical confrontation with one of the bigger male aides. I don't think I was thinking that I could take him on, as he was much bigger and stronger than me; however, before I knew it, they put me in some sort of straitjacket. I was put in a room with only one very small window in the door, and they laid me down on a table. I was not able to move my hands or legs. Then the staff left and locked me in there. I did not like this at all, and claustrophobia was getting the better of me. I knew this was not quite the attention I was trying to seek. I remember lying there and deciding I was going to be like Houdini, and I convinced myself I could get my arms free. Somehow I did!

I really felt like I outsmarted them. When they came to take off the restraints, they were surprised to find I had removed them myself. My reaction was, "Great, I got them!" I never really quite understood why they thought they had to go to those measures; I may have put up more of a fight than I remember. Nevertheless, being restrained in that manner was a very scary experience for me. Later, someone on staff said that they were afraid I really was going to hurt myself. Maybe they *had* noticed the cut on my arm. As I recall, when patients were on suicide watch, someone from the staff sat outside their room all night. I think the thought of that type of attention was what I was seeking, because it comforted me—but who knows? My mind was not working properly.

I made some new friends with fellow patients on the outpatient unit, and I became especially close to one, Ruth. Having people who really cared about me in there made a difference. Ruth also happened to be a nurse at this very hospital, on a different unit, and her credentials ultimately saved me from what could have been a very serious physical complication. While hospitalized, I had been given some medication and was put on a high-dose birth control pill, because I never completely stopped bleeding after the abortion; it had been six weeks since the procedure. I could not get the nurses to help me to do anything about the bleeding, because they all said they were too busy due to the Thanksgiving holiday. I could not believe this—it was a hospital, for heaven's sake! Perhaps they got tired of false alarms and overreactive patients in the psych unit. Anyway, they did not know with whom they were dealing.

Ruth stepped in. She knew just how the system worked there and could point me in the right direction. We had the on-call surgeon paged, and he paid a visit to me and scheduled me to have a D and C a few days later. As I had been insisting, something was not totally right with the abortion that was performed. I still thought it was done too early. The doctor was not thrilled that the nurses in the psychiatric unit had not helped me. I was pleasantly satisfied that I was able to get this help myself, through Ruth. I thought it was pretty clever. This was just a reminder of how often one has to be one's own advocate, although that should not have been the case in this type of situation. Ruth and I developed a very strong relationship as a result of our illnesses and remained friends for some time; I was actually in her wedding party a couple years later. Once again, something positive came out of a very uncomfortable and difficult situation.

I remember reading from my old Bible I had received from my parents when I was confirmed; they must have brought it in for me, and I probably requested it. I did not read the Bible on a regular basis, but I found it comforting while in the hospital. I was by myself in my room and began to read from it. I was reading the words printed in red for the words that Jesus spoke, and a very peculiar thing happened: I was somehow able to speak the words without actually looking at the text. At this point, I was feeling as if the Holy Spirit was working through me; it was similar to my first hospitalization, when I was with my dad in the chapel. To this day that baffles me. My memory is very clear on that, because I remember after reading for a while how interesting that was—I was there, but not really. It appeared as if I were reading the words, but I wasn't; the words were coming from a higher power, inspired through me. It was as if I was not really part of this world. Remembering this helps me more and more to see the aspects of God throughout this illness; I just never put it all together. As with my first hospitalization, I was feeling very close to God. It has been said that many bipolar patients, when in a manic episode, experience a form of spirituality, sometimes even to the extreme of feeling like you are Christ himself, but to this day I am not convinced that it is only due to the illness. It still could be an extension of who I already was.

There was a psychiatric aide named Jeff who was of great comfort to me during this hospitalization. Jeff was in training to be some type of counselor, and he was such a caring individual and a great listener. He loaned me a book while I was there titled *When Bad Things Happen to Good People* by Harold S. Kushner. Once again my concentration wasn't all that good, so he ended up letting me keep it. I have held on to that book to this day, and I still remember some of our conversations. I also remember him really trying to understand me, my illness, and all that had happened to me. Jeff knew that many people with mood disorders have dysfunctional families and traumatic childhoods. He asked me many questions, and he finally realized this was not the case with me. This was over twenty years ago, and so much more has been discovered about this illness since then, especially the fact that bipolar disorder is a genetic and biological disorder, and one that is not necessarily derived from a dysfunctional past. I'm quite sure Jeff learned a lot from me during that month. I know I learned a lot from him, especially in how he treated me with kindness and compassion without judgment.

During this hospitalization, I also had a really difficult time coming to terms with the decision to terminate the life of my unborn child. Knowing I did not really have a choice about keeping the baby was somewhat comforting, but only to a degree. I did not think it was fair for me to feel okay about it just because I was instructed to do it. I continued to punish myself for my decision and to accept full blame. When I tried to suppress the enormity of the emotional ramifications, in the beginning it just did not work; this was surely the reason I found myself in the hospital not too long after. I had been through some very difficult times, but ending this life was certainly the most difficult thing I had ever been through, and in my mind it was wrong, whether or not I had a good enough reason. I have worked on accepting God's forgiveness, but forgiving myself took a very long time.

Once I was discharged from the hospital and had regained my coping skills to make it in the outside world, I returned to my student employee's job; they were great to keep it for me after being gone a full month. I tried to manage four classes and had to decide, once again, if I would take incompletes or drop them. I met with each professor as well as a department advisor at Pitt. I was struggling before the month-long hospitalization with this course load, and during all the chaos my coursework had suffered. I decided to drop two of my classes and complete the other two. Soon it would be Christmas break, and by January I was more than ready for a fresh start. All of this happened in the fall; the pattern continued to emerge that autumn would prove to be a difficult time of year for me from that time forward.

For the most part, I endured the same aftereffects from this manic episode and hospitalization as I had before. Rebuilding my confidence never got any easier, even though the feelings were not foreign to me. Also, while coming down from this manic episode there was so much more at stake: the date rape, the pregnancy, and the abortion. The reality of what I shared with others while manic haunted me, especially the abortion. In a nonmanic state I would have been much more discreet. Lastly, this manic episode included deeper emotional ramifications *not* related to the illness.

Chapter 5
I Need a Time-Out: Hospitalization #4

I ONCE AGAIN EXPERIENCED almost two years without incident in terms of my bipolar illness. For all intents and purposes, I was doing very well with most aspects of my illness. I continued my routine with part-time work and full-time study, both at the University of Pittsburgh. By the time school started up again in August 1989, my lease was up, and I moved back in with my parents.

After a college friend and I returned from a week-long excursion to Los Angeles (it was supposed to be for the whole summer, but because we could not find jobs, we cut the trip short), I was given the opportunity to interview for a full-time position at Pitt, which would carry the benefit of essentially covering all tuition costs for school.

I was offered a job as the secretary for the department of neuroscience. After returning from the "trip gone wrong," I felt ready to make the commitment to a permanent, full-time position. Had I not gone on this trip in the first place and quickly returned when I did, my life would have taken a different direction for so many reasons. I would now be able to pay for the majority of what was left for my tuition to obtain a degree. The employee tuition benefit meant paying only $5.00 per credit, which not only gave me a sense of responsibility but also made me feel good to be accountable for the financial part of my education. The change to full-time work and part-time school also resulted in higher academic scores. I learned that this type of rigorous routine worked well for me, and that a structured environment enhanced my sense of balance and productivity.

Although I certainly saw many positives in my new situation, I couldn't help but acknowledge that I had the illness to thank for subsequently ending up so behind in life. Many of my friends had already graduated from college, appeared to have great jobs, and lived on their own. It took me some time to realize that this was my life I was living, and I shouldn't compare myself to anyone else—not always an easy thing to do.

It wasn't until November 1990 that I began to recognize some familiar symptoms, despite being on my regular medication, lithium. I noticed how easily stressed and overwhelmed I was becoming. My ability to focus was diminishing, and I could feel my coping skills slipping away. My classes became increasingly more difficult. I was feeling some of the same warning signs of mania—less sleep, racing thoughts, increased confusion—that preceded the first three hospitalizations. On top of all this, I was also very involved as a bridesmaid for a good friend's wedding, just one more thing that contributed to the spiraling of this episode.

Recognizing the warning signs and knowing the potential outcome if not addressed, I had it all arranged that I would go into the hospital the day after my friend's wedding. I think my psychiatrist felt I was too with it this time, especially when I had planned it, as if I was making a reservation for a hotel. I felt that going in the hospital was a very wise decision for me to make while I still had some control, as opposed to waiting until it was too late. My psychiatrist made it clear to me that she felt she could not hospitalize me unless I was a danger to myself or others.

Because my doctor did not think I needed the hospital, and she was out of town, I lied and told the doctor on call that I was in danger of hurting myself. I knew that doing this was the only way in, and it was the only way I knew how to get help. I really did not know of any other option but to check out from everything. I went to what I knew I needed; to me, help meant to go to the hospital where I would be safe. Looking back, I probably could have just used a time-out for a week or so, but I did not know how to do that on my own.

This hospitalization was pretty unremarkable in that it only lasted ten days. I went to St. Francis Hospital, where I had been before, and voluntarily checked myself into the psychiatric unit—though come

48

to think of it, I have never resisted an admission. I don't think this notion of wanting to be hospitalized is so common, especially when in a manic episode. I initially saw the same attending psychiatrist I'd met with for the 1988 hospitalization. I made the following notes to share with him to let him know why I was there and just how I was feeling.

- Thoughts okay so far, but a little racing—trying to slow them down
- Trying to think before I speak
- Nervous more
- Scared to be alone—feel safe in hospital
- Physically and mentally exhausted
- Crying way too much
- Can't seem to cope/function too well in the "real" world
- Current psychiatrist said I was rapid cycling
- Extremely irritable and very impatient

The attending psychiatrist was impressed with how much I had matured since my hospitalization two years prior; I think I was in a different state of mind the last time he'd seen me. It was a bit troublesome how nice he was to me now that I was functioning better. Treating a patient in such a completely different manner was not acceptable to me. I could not help the way I was responding before due to my illness, and as a professional in this field, he could have been just as understanding and compassionate the first time around. To me, it was as if he was treating me with kindness as a payoff for my good behavior.

We talked about my studies, and I let him know about the research paper I had just written on teenage suicide. He was very interested and asked if he could borrow a copy. He later gave it back to me with a note, thanking me and letting me know he'd presented it at a meeting to a professor of psychiatry at the Department of Psychiatry (Child and Adolescent Program) at Western Psychiatric Institute and Clinic of the University of Pittsburgh Medical Center. I sensed the attending psychiatrist was taken with the quality of my paper, and that made me feel good.

Again, this fourth hospitalization was very easy in comparison to the first three, and I did not need much help.

My journal entries from this time in the hospital show what was running through my head during a "not so bad" episode. While hospitalized, I wrote the following:

Monday, November 19, 1990
5:20 a.m.

Current Thoughts:

So far much better than when I was here the first time two years ago exactly—probably because I'm not so goofy.

Hospitals take some of my fears away—e.g., fear of being alone. Maybe that's why I like them so much— basically I feel safe.

Need to sleep a good six to eight hours here. Last night went to bed at 1:00 a.m. and was up with a sore throat at 5:00 a.m. (not good). Gargled, still hurts—oh well, what can you do?

Met some interesting people, but can't remember names too well, yet. Oh no—there goes my memory again! Ha ha! It's wild, the woman next door to me was next door to me at Jefferson Hospital (3/84), and here we are six years, eight months later, next-door neighbors again. Wow, what a small world.

It's 5:30—I have to wait till 6:00 to leave this room. Me, up this early— imagine that!

Well this is enough of this for now!

My next journal entry was as follows:

Friday, November 23, 1990
6:45 a.m.

Current Thoughts:

I feel that I have learned more about myself and my illness this week. Over the course of six years that I have been diagnosed bipolar or manic-depressive, I have researched a great deal on my own, mainly because I am very important to myself and realize the importance of educating me on an illness I have been labeled with.

This week in particular I learned things I knew not too much about—through myself and others.

- *I learned that no matter how bad I feel, I will get better.*
- *By recognizing the signs more clearly, I have taken the correct measure in seeking out help.*
- *By joining a support group I have found a very special group of people—all of who have experienced in some way what I have.*
- *By becoming actively involved in other areas within the National Depressive and Manic-Depressive Association (NDMDA), I can potentially help others while representing my support group.*
- *I always seem to give the credit of my getting better to my doctor, medicine, friends, and family. Although I realize they have added to my recoveries, I now feel that along with God's help, I too am a major contributor to my treatment. In other words, I'm giving myself a pat on the back for once.*

- *I've learned I am a true fighter (all six years, including getting through school, etc.), and I will never stop that fight.*
- *Very important—*
  - *I am very proud of myself for having the power to feel like I do at this very moment, when the past six weeks have been not so good, especially this past week.*
  - *I learned that just because I'm feeling things I felt when I was hospitalized before does not mean I must go in the hospital (but that is what I associate it with).*
  - *Everybody has depression, mood swings, and euphoric feelings at times—mine are just manifested differently, and I need a little extra help (therapy and meds to control them).*

These writings are a good indicator that something was unusual with my thought processes, but it was not extreme or a full-blown mania.

One disturbing and potentially very dangerous experience during this hospitalization involved a staff aide. Although I was not experiencing full-blown mania this time, I certainly had some issues and was very vulnerable. I also automatically assumed that all staff were safe and there to help rather than to take advantage of the patients.

There was a psychiatric aide who worked on the floor where my room was located. He was about forty-five years old, and I was twenty-four and felt we had some sort of connection. In that short stay, the staff aide and I developed a strong liking toward one another, and he slipped me his phone number right before I was discharged. This was totally inappropriate, but of course I did not see it that way and I was happy about it. Since I was back living at home, my parents knew what was going on, and they thought it was wrong, but as per my usual strong-willed self, I convinced them this was totally okay and that he really liked me. We went out on several dates, and I know my parents continued to be concerned, but they really could not stop me. It wasn't like I was still a teenager.

My parents' instincts proved to be correct, and he soon broke off the relationship, saying he could not give me the attention I deserved. He told me he decided he had too much on his plate between his daughter from a previous marriage, his development project, and the work he was doing at the hospital. (This seemed a little shady—why was he working as a psychiatric aide when he had this big development project going on? It just did not add up to me.) In the end, I was very hurt and saddened because my feelings had continued to grow for him, and he provided some sort of comfort to me so I felt close to him. He also had been a support while I was vulnerable and having a difficult time in the hospital, and I had formed an attachment to him. I was very naïve and not totally well, either. I'm still not really sure about the hospital's regulations, but somehow I believe it was not in the policy and procedure manual to start dating the patients on the psychiatric floor. An incident like this should have been reported, but I did not have the judgment to realize this was not right at the time. Had I met him in a different situation, I am sure I would not have been interested in him at all. As I look back, I recall there was something a little off with him, but at the time I could not detect it. It is truly very scary to think of what can go on in the lives of people who have psychiatric disorders. The world is not safe enough to begin with, and especially so when you don't have all your faculties. It is too easy to take advantage of someone in this type of situation.

With this last hospitalization, I was out of work for about two weeks. I did not really have any thought about how my job would be filled while I was out. Everything gets put on hold until one starts to get better, and then one returns to the concerns of ongoing reality. My supervisor asked one of our undergraduates who was working in one of the labs to fill in for me. My absence did not seem to be a problem. Most did not know exactly why I was out, but the graduate students and professors were all very concerned about me. One of the graduate students came to visit, others called, and they all signed a group card for me. No one asked me questions when I returned; they were simply very supportive and happy that I was back. It was a pretty great thing that they kept me, especially considering I had only been working there for four months.

This hospitalization lasted through Thanksgiving (not fun to be there over a holiday again) and is to date—and hopefully forever—my last hospitalization. As time passed, with the support of my doctors and my increasing awareness, I began to return to the feelings of normalcy that I desired. Throughout the good times, I continued to discover what situations worked well for me, and how facing and acknowledging aspects of this illness would continue to support my health and well-being. However, when one is in the challenging times of mania or struggling with side effects, it feels all-consuming. It is at those times, in the thick of the episode or when experiencing its aftereffects (mania, chaos, loss of control, and hospitalization, and then dealing with peoples' reactions after the fact, picking up the pieces, getting back on schedule with feeling behind, and building up that lost self-esteem) that one believes one will always feel this way. To this day, when my coping skills start to diminish, I begin to get concerned and try to take the appropriate precautions to prevent it from moving forward.

It took this hospitalization for me to realize that I could feel safe and manage the precursors of mania before the warning signs turned into a full-blown manic episode, without needing the security provided by the hospital. I had now lived with my illness for six years. The main change was that I had experience with the illness, had taken time to make some sense of it, and had gained a better understanding of it so that I was able to catch it early. I also still had my medication on board, which was very important. This episode showed me that I had a better handle on the illness as a whole. I could and would continue to take ownership of the illness and the responsibilities that came along with it to manage my bipolar disorder the best I could.

Chapter 6
The Golden Years: Life without Episodes

LITTLE DID I KNOW that the next ten years, from December 1990 to August 2000, would be such wonderful years. Aside from minor ups and downs, my life was free of any severe manic episodes. I did have occasional bouts of hypomania where I was more productive, more organized, and had more energy than usual; it was during these times I had a little taste of that high I so loved. I was now aware of the nature of a hypomanic state but did not allow them to compromise my health. I knew the warning signs and took the measures I had come to know to prevent the hypomania from escalating into full-blown mania.

During these golden years I experienced a level of normalcy that was present prior to my first manic episode at age seventeen. I was now twenty-four and was worry-free in dealing with the illness as long as I continued medication compliance and the other protocols that I had set in place. The illness was no longer an all-consuming part of my daily living, and the devastating disruptions in my life ceased. It was during these years I truly enjoyed living. Anyone who got to know me during this time or met me on the street would never have known that I had bipolar disorder and how I had struggled with it for the previous six years. This brought me great joy.

I credit Dr. Scott Gleditsch, the first psychiatrist to treat me as an inpatient during my first hospitalization in 1984, for encouraging me to consider trying the medication Tegretol (generic name

Carbamazepine), which improved my quality of life significantly throughout those ten years. Dr. Gleditsch happened to be a member of the church my family attended, and he knew of my continued struggles with this illness during the past few years while in college.

Back in the summer of 1990 (and prior to my fourth hospitalization), Dr. Gleditsch took me aside after church. He talked to me in the gentle voice of his that had a way of making things so calm. He informed me that psychiatrists were now utilizing Tegretol (originally approved by the Food and Drug Administration for epilepsy) for bipolar disorder as a mood stabilizer. He told me that with Tegretol, I would require blood level checks (as I did with lithium) because Tegretol needed to be monitored even more carefully; the therapeutic range was only documented for epilepsy.

Although I mentioned Tegretol to my current psychiatrist that summer, I was a little scared to try a new medication with the possibility of side effects and the even closer watch of my blood levels. At that time I decided not to go on Tegretol because I felt I was doing just fine, so why would I start a new medication and risk rocking the boat?

Within six months of Dr. Gleditsch's recommendation—and after my fourth hospitalization—I decided enough was enough. Scared or not, I was going to start the Tegretol. I was convinced I needed more help.

Tegretol became an important medication to add to my treatment regimen because I had been taken off lithium by my psychiatrist at Michigan State University in January 1985. This was approximately eight months after starting it, thus initiating what we believe to be my refractory response to lithium. I was informed that a refractory response is when a patient is taken off a medication (for me, lithium) and then when it is reintroduced to the patient, this same medication either is not as efficacious or does not work the same way. It is often necessary to introduce additional medications to regain stabilization.

I am constantly reminded of how important it is to work with a competent doctor—in my case, a doctor who understands the complexity of medications required for bipolar disorder and the ramifications that result when it is not fully understood. Many people who experience this disorder will at one time be exposed to lithium. If a person experiences this refractory response to lithium, it could possibly dictate their mood stabilization for the rest of his or her life.

I also continued to regularly attend a support group that met weekly. The support group was for both depression and manic depression, and there were anywhere from ten to thirty people there each night. Being part of this group brought great comfort to me: at certain times I needed the help from the group, and at other times I was there to give it; such exchanges are the basis of a support group. To be with others who actually knew what I was going through made a difference; I felt safe, and it helped me to realize that I was not alone.

I became a member of the board of our area chapter of the National Depressive and Manic-Depressive Association (NDMDA), now known as the Depression and Bipolar Support Alliance (DBSA). Our support group hosted local speakers who would come to give informational presentations, including Ellen Frank, PhD (who now is on the board of directors for DBSA and internationally recognized for her work on mood disorders). The NDMDA would also sponsor nationally known speakers who would present at the University of Pittsburgh.

We also had some not-so-well-known people give informative talks to the support group. One time I was asked to lead the group. I had done much research on the illness and had gained enough understanding to feel confident to share my knowledge. It was important for me to know everything possible about this illness that I had. Now that I was in a stable environment with my medication, job, school, and social life, I had gained valuable perspective and desired to be a support to others.

I still have my notes from my April 1991 talk, and it is amazing to me all the thoughts, ideas, and suggestions I had back then. Basically they are the same strategies I try to live by today. The title of my discussion was "Striving at Staying Well, or Ways to Make Yourself Feel Better When Not Well."

Overview
- It is important to express the normalcy of our illness as opposed to thinking it is so abnormal.
- There are so many people with illnesses related to depression—I think that sometimes we feel we are the only ones who have it.
- Everyone has problems. We must realize that our unipolar, bipolar, or whatever illness we possess is merely our illness and we must go on living.
- Although at times it may have to, our illness should not encompass our entire lives. We need to focus more on other facets of our lives.
- I do believe that we should educate ourselves as much as we can—at least to have a good understanding of what our illness is and how it affects us—but sometimes people tend to become too wrapped up in their illness by doing so.

Certain measures I take in order to stay well
1. Maintain a routine. Anything you do, do it with some regularity. This includes sleep (what time you go to bed and wake up). Try to do this at the same time whenever possible. Also make sure to get enough sleep—whatever you feel you need (or what your doctor has told you).
2. Eat a healthy diet and do not skip meals.
3. Exercise three to four times per week, which should help you to feel better and more energetic.
4. Limit your caffeine intake.
5. Limit alcohol consumption and, if possible, cut it out altogether. Alcohol is a depressant, so why take that risk?
6. Comply with medication regimens.
7. Truly do what your doctor advises.

Although each item alone may not seem to have much effect on the way we feel, when combined, the results can be really great.

Things that are unhealthy for our illnesses

1. Feeling sorry for ourselves is one of the worst things we can do. We somehow have to learn how to recognize when the signs of either a mania or depressive episode are coming on. I feel we are all guilty of ignoring these signs or feeling sorry for ourselves when the signs appear. For me, I come to a point where I realize that it's not getting me anywhere; I'm just like anyone else with a problem. Yes, mania or depression is a different kind of problem or illness, but it is *my* problem, and I need to deal with it.

2. Sometimes I feel that my illness prohibits me from doing certain things or reaching certain goals. Instead of giving up, I need to fight. I just know that I may have to work harder than others or harder than I had to in the past. Again, it's not anybody else's problem but my own. I realize with any mood disorder this can be very difficult, but I have to hold on to hope. I may not see instant results, but in time I feel I can still achieve what I want. Personally, I have to push myself; if not, I will not go anywhere.

3. Our attitudes seem to play a major role in our ability to stay well. If you have it in your mind that you are sick and cannot get better, you won't. You must somehow achieve a positive attitude. I realize this can seem close to impossible at times.

4. When times are so low, you must look at the many individuals who are worse off than yourself. This should give you a sense of perspective.

5. When problems seem to build up, try to treat them as smaller individual issues instead of one huge thing—like *everything* is wrong.

6. Not accepting that you have an illness makes the battle twice as hard. You won't be able to be fully treated until you do this.

Sharing very personal stories was extremely important to the support of all who attended. The ones who had experienced mania all had experiences that were common in some way. Many shared extravagant spending sprees, including one woman who had purchased a new car, rented a limo, and checked into a very exclusive hotel thinking she would start living there. People had outrageous affairs, destroying marriages and families. While manic, most talked very fast with racing thoughts, and some even experienced hallucinations. Together we laughed, cried, listened, and shared whatever we felt at a given time. We would also have some nights for families to attend. It was very beneficial for many. I truly believe in these types of groups.

One thing I realized as a result of attending this group was that it was difficult for me to get too close to any one person there, because this was not my life, just a part of it. I feared allowing the illness to consume my life. With all the involvement I had and the research I was doing, I realized I needed to pull back a bit and stay focused on getting on with other things in my life. At the time, this was a wise decision for me.

I continued working full-time in the neuroscience department and attended school part-time for the next three years. Working forty-hour weeks provided the crux of my structure and stability. Incorporating this type of scheduled routine taught me that I thrived in this type of lifestyle and was most successful when I lived in this manner.

Additionally, I loved the social aspect of this job. I was located in the front office, so I was the first person everyone would see when they came for their mail, coffee, or the copy machine, and also when the professors came by to give me work. Multiple times each day, someone (most likely a graduate student or lab technician) would sit down in a chair adjacent to my desk and start to talk. I often felt as if I had a sign up that read, "The doctor is in." I loved that others felt comfortable telling me their problems or excitement and all their updates. Engaging personally in the work environment increased my job satisfaction.

I enjoyed many social activities with friends during this time and attended professional sporting events (Pirates, Steelers, and Penguins games), as well as Pitt basketball games. I traveled with friends to the Caribbean on several occasions. I was regularly physically active with swimming, aerobics, and walking or running the track. Almost every Friday, it was happy hour in downtown Pittsburgh. I loved seeing so many people and could not get enough of it. I was carefree and normal and enjoyed just living like others.

In May 1994 I graduated from the University of Pittsburgh with a bachelor of arts degree in sociology and a minor in psychology. My parents had a graduation party for me, and about sixty friends and family attended. My invitation said, "Come Help Celebrate the End of a Decade." Graduation was a very proud moment for me after all I had been through. It was a long ten years. Although it was not an easy road, I had attained my goal through perseverance and belief in myself. Also, financing a large portion of my education on my own gave me an extra sense of accomplishment.

Obtaining my degree would have been much more difficult without the support of my parents. They allowed me to live at home those years, and financially I did not have to worry about anything except my car and personal items. My parents believed in me and supported my decisions to move forward to pursue what I was going after. I think any parent would want this for their child, but in my situation I think it could have been easy for my parents to be more protective and encourage me not to push myself. My parents did not ever treat me as a person with a mental illness, but as a person, period. That kind of support was an essential component to my well-being.

I continued to work full-time throughout the summer and took the GRE in the fall of 1994. I took a prep class prior to taking the test because it had been so long since I had taken a standardized test, and historically I had difficulty with these types of exams. I then applied to two out-of-state universities to pursue a master's degree in social work. In February 1995 I got the news I did not get accepted to either school, and initially it was a big disappointment. I did get past that, and because I desired a change in my life, I began to be on the lookout for new opportunities. Ultimately, I felt that if graduate school was meant to be, it would happen at some other point in time.

That summer, while still working full-time at Pitt, I decided to get some experience in the social work and counseling field. After many background clearances, I started a part-time job as a substitute counselor for boys who lived in group homes and had been sexually abused. The knowledge I gained from that short-lived job was more than I ever expected. These boys suffered unimaginable abuse—and mostly by family members or someone they knew. I came to understand it wasn't just about the sexual act; it was about the control of the abuser and the shame experienced by the victim. The sexual abuse affected all areas of their lives and would most likely haunt them for years to come, if not forever. I was overcome with compassion for these boys. Unfortunately, there was only so much I could do for them, but hopefully it meant something just to have someone who cared about them without presenting a threat. This experience added tremendously to my already increasing desire to serve those in need in some capacity.

Around that same time I had lunch with my friend Erin, from the neuroscience department at Pitt. Erin told me she would be moving to Washington, DC, to continue working for the physician she was assisting at the University of Pittsburgh. She would be running her physician's lab in the division of endocrinology at Georgetown University Medical Center. As we talked about her future plans, I started to ask what her thoughts were about me moving with her. I only got out, "Do you think ...?"

Before I even finished the question, Erin said, "Say no more— yes!" Erin knew I was interested in making a change, and I was amazed and pleased she was able to read my thoughts so quickly.

Although I had many friends in Pittsburgh, I also knew my parents would be retiring the next year to Southern Pines, North Carolina. I was open to moving from the city I had grown to love, and exploring new opportunities appealed to me.

Other key factors played a role in precipitating my desire to make a big change. A serious relationship had just ended, and sitting around and sulking was not a good option for me. I believed that if the right situation presented itself, something new and exciting would help move me forward in a positive direction. I also felt I was at an age that if I waited any longer, I might never have the gumption to get up and leave everything.

I began researching jobs in the DC area, and before I knew it, Erin had an interview set up for me in the same department she would be working in, at Georgetown University Medical Center. It was fortunate that there was a position open and Erin needed a roommate. The situation could not have presented itself more perfectly.

I then went to Washington, DC, for the Fourth of July to visit Erin, and while I was there had a formal interview at Georgetown University Medical Center's department of endocrinology. I was pretty confident I got the job. My only concern was that I was not sure the DC area was where I wanted to be. Having visited several times before, I was well aware of the frustration I would experience with all the traffic. I also felt the Georgetown area was a collegiate town—a bit young for me, because I was twenty-nine—and I did not get the best feel from it. After spending the weekend with Erin, she sensed I would probably turn the opportunity down. After weighing the pros and cons, my gut feeling was telling me to go because the pros (job offer, roommate, place to live, new beginning without too many risks, my brother living nearby) outweighed the cons. It seemed as if I was being led in the direction of moving to Washington, DC, and the timing was right.

My friends were pretty surprised to hear the news. I had kept it quiet and waited until I had secured the job and finalized my decision to move before I shared it with anyone. It all happened so quickly, and it was difficult to say good-bye to them, but I was excited to start this new chapter of my life.

I moved on August 5, 1995. It was an emotional day and bittersweet. I had so much I was leaving behind in Pittsburgh, yet so much was in front of me. I was happy that I had met my goal of moving out of my parents' home prior to being forced out when they retired. That was important to me, and I was ready to go.

After the four-and-a-half-hour drive to Northern Virginia from Pittsburgh, I arrived at my brother's place, where I would be staying for the first few weeks. He and his wife were on their honeymoon, so it was quite challenging starting totally alone, even though I knew it was for just one week until they returned. I found myself a bit lonely at first. I started working immediately and had a two-hour commute from Alexandria to Georgetown via car, metro, and shuttle bus. It was quite an experience, especially considering my start time was 8:00 a.m. I kept reminding myself that this was only for three weeks until I would be living in Rosslyn, which would really lessen the commute.

While working at Georgetown and during my first year in the Washington, DC, area (1995–1996), I made some new friends, dated a few men, went out quite a bit, and traveled when I could. I was managing my illness quite well through the 1990s, trying to take care of myself the best I could, and life was pretty great. The only real illness-related negative that ran concurrent during my golden years was that I was not thrilled with my psychiatric treatment while working at Georgetown. I had two insurance options to choose from: a health management organization (HMO) or the Georgetown Health Plan. I chose the HMO because I feared someone at work would find out about my illness.

My last psychiatrist in Pittsburgh recommended that I see an internist for medications and blood level checks rather than another psychiatrist. He thought yearly checks would be sufficient because I had been doing it that way for several years, and my lithium level was well controlled. I was unable to follow his advice because the primary care physician at my new HMO did not feel comfortable treating bipolar disorder and referred me to a psychiatrist within the HMO's system. Further, with this HMO I had to see whatever psychiatrist was available the day of my appointment. Having a rotating treatment provider was tough because I was seeing a variety of doctors and could not establish a real relationship with any of them. As one can imagine, the doctor-patient relationship is essential with these types of illnesses.

As a consequence of not having the established doctor-patient relationship, at one of my rotating appointments I saw a psychiatrist who was straight out of residency. She was not aware that one of my medications (Tegretol) could interfere with the effectiveness of birth control pills. This psychiatrist actually asked *me* to bring *her* the information. I could not believe that she would not do a search on something of this nature—not just for me, but in consideration for her other patients as well. For a patient to get pregnant while taking birth control pills could be devastating—especially due to the risk of birth defects associated with both Tegretol and lithium. I hope she discovered the consequences of this connection later.

One of the benefits of working at Georgetown was free tuition for any classes taken. I was now also considering law school and decided to pursue the one-year paralegal program in the fall of 1996. Taking on this program was a very positive experience and challenged me to structure my time between work and school as well as engaging my mind to learn something new. This type of regimen had proved to be beneficial in the past. I knew that keeping on this type of schedule and staying busy worked well for me, allowing me to be more organized than when I was not involved in so much. I also continued to discover how important it was for me to engage myself in some form of educational experience outside of work. Continuing to stimulate my brain and work toward accomplishing a goal has always been important to me. It also helps me to keep the mundane and boredom factor out of my life. I also made some great friends during the program.

I spent many weekends during the summer of 1997 at a group beach house that my roommate and I belonged to in Dewey Beach, Delaware. It was a lot of fun, yet many of those weekends I would also attempt to study for the paralegal program I was taking at Georgetown University, while sitting on the beach in my chair. I had now officially become one of the Washington, DC, summer weekenders.

In addition to that, I was a mentor for an eleven-year-old girl who was part of a group home in Alexandria, Virginia. She had been both physically and emotionally abused by her mother and could not live in her own home. We spent lots of time together. I really enjoyed sharing my time with her and providing some sense of stability in her life, even if for a brief period. The mentoring ended after about eight months, when she moved to be with her father in Atlanta. We continued to be in contact for a few years, but then I lost track of her. Gosh, I felt awful for her. This was another experience leading me toward my quest to help others, but hopefully through a full-time position, not just volunteering.

In August 1997, I left the division of endocrinology and took a job in hospital administration at Georgetown Hospital as a credentials coordinator. To sum it up, this job was really a way of checking the doctors' legitimacy (verifying all their past educational history, licenses, etc.) to enable them to have hospital privileges. Being the only credentials coordinator was a huge challenge because I was walking into a mess. The job required an excessive amount of attention to the smallest of details. I was told this was a difficult position to fill because many people didn't like such detail-oriented responsibilities. I, however, jumped at the chance to dive in and organize it all. I love a good challenge, and in time I was able to make the office run the way it was intended. There were so many new physicians coming on board that they hired an assistant for me. Once the assistant was trained and up to speed, things worked smoothly, and soon I became bored and not satisfied overall with my job at Georgetown.

Sensing and hearing about my current lack of job satisfaction, a new roommate encouraged me to fax my resume to her sister, who was a manager at a contracting company for pharmaceuticals. Her sister thought that this career might be a good fit for me. For some reason I had been told this by quite a few other people. I was hired by this company in May of 1999. They contracted with a larger pharmaceutical company whose products I would be promoting. The hiring process went quickly, and in about two weeks I was on my way to a new, exciting endeavor. Little did I know that this would be the beginning of a career that would last more than ten years.

New healthcare benefits accompanied the job; this meant a new psychiatrist. I was unhappy with the revolving schedule of psychiatrists with my previous insurer, so I was hoping to find one doctor I would see on a regular basis. Within a few months I found a doctor who was in network.

After working for this contracting company for nine months, with the support of my manager, I was recommended and then hired to work directly for the larger pharmaceutical company whose products I had already been promoting. I was interviewed and hired in March 2000.

The pharmaceutical sales position with this company offered challenges I did not have with the other company. Taking this new position with new products and a new territory certainly gave me the challenge I was missing. Working directly for the larger pharmaceutical company gave me more to do—much more. I went from having too much time on my hands to no time at all. I participated in more than three weeks of training to prepare for the transition, and the early months in this new position were extremely hectic while I got acclimated to my new territory and products. In addition to sales calls, at that time we did a lot of entertaining, including dinner programs, football games, basketball games, and shows with my customers. There were so many evenings and weekend days out. It was not what I wanted, although it appeared to be appealing to those around me. I would have preferred to be with friends and family, and to see the events on my own time. Working so many hours coupled with the entertainment component made achieving my goal of keeping balance very difficult, but I was managing the best I could.

Looking back over the course of this decade, I was functioning quite well. Although I was very aware of my illness and the responsibilities to maintain my health and wellness, I was simply free to live and enjoy my life. I did not have to deal with or focus on all that came along with the illness.

Unfortunately, after this ten-year span of relative ease with my illness, the swings of bipolar disorder soon returned. I knew this was always a possibility, so I treasure those years, knowing how fortunate I was.

Chapter 7
Opening Pandora's Box: Introduction to Depression

OPENING PANDORA'S BOX IS my experience of the opposing extreme of mania: clinical depression (also known as major depression). Once again, the notion of normalcy I had fought to obtain was left behind.

Up until August 2000, I had only experienced the aftermath of the highs of the mania, which for me are in and of themselves a form of depression—but not to the extreme extent of what I perceive as clinical depression. Clinical depression is not situational depression. Situational depression occurs as a response to external circumstances and typically subsides when the stressor has been alleviated; however, if a situational depression persists, it can turn into clinical depression. Experiencing and surviving a clinical depression is devastating, and for many it is difficult to fully comprehend. Although it can be triggered by a traumatic event, clinical depression is not about being sad; it is the result of a chemical imbalance that then causes the symptoms of depression.

The year prior to August 2000, I was once again seeing only one psychiatrist. When I had my initial consultation with this new psychiatrist back in 1999, I was stabilized and still on my same regimen of lithium and Tegretol, however I was also feeling a bit flat and sluggish. We both agreed that I could benefit from an antidepressant that would not only work as an energizer but would also aid in focusing. I knew by this time that I was very sensitive to medication, and I mentioned this to the psychiatrist. He started me on the antidepressant Wellbutrin to help with the issues I had shared with him.

I began with a very small dosage, a mere 37.5 mg (the normal starting dose was 100 mg at that time). Very quickly I felt as if I was going to jump out of my skin, and I discontinued the Wellbutrin immediately after discussing the reaction with my psychiatrist. I discovered that the psychiatrist had prescribed an older form of Wellbutrin, the immediate release formulation (IR), which enters into the system much more quickly than the newer sustained release formulation (SR). Because I had been promoting Wellbutrin SR for my job, I knew that Wellbutrin IR had not been promoted for years. I had read about, seen data, and heard from physicians that Wellbutrin SR worked well for many people, and I believed it to be an efficacious medication. However, because of my reaction to it, I decided I was better off not only to stop the Wellbutrin, but also to stay with the medication I was currently taking rather than try another antidepressant that could lead to disturbing side effects.

After realizing that this psychiatrist must have made a mistake, I was quite disappointed. My initial thought regarding this psychiatrist was that he did not seem to be up-to-date on the latest research for bipolar disorder, and so with this simple error, I lost even more confidence in him. I understand we are all human, but I also feel that this situation could have been avoided had he known more about the new formulation of Wellbutrin SR—or perhaps it was his simple error in not writing "SR" next to Wellbutrin; if Wellbutrin alone is written on the prescription, then the IR version is automatically dispensed.

This experience reminded me of the patient's responsibility to stay on top of medication treatment plans instead of following the natural inclination to completely trust the knowledge of one's doctor. Based on my history and the various levels of competence with which my illness has been treated, I feel it is imperative that I, and others with mental illness, receive the most up-to-date information. Treatment protocol most often includes a prescribed medication that affects brain chemistry; this in turn affects thoughts and behaviors of the individual patient and may spill over to everything that impacts their lives. The behavioral consequences of medication prescribed can be positive or negative, and careful attention needs to be given when treating mental illness. In my particular case, I assumed my psychiatrist was prescribing me the right formulation and did not question it. I don't think I even thought about researching it any further because I trusted him.

Several months after the Wellbutrin mix-up, I helped to plan a lecture given by a psychiatrist in Washington, DC. Coordinating speaker programs for customers was a responsibility of my pharmaceutical sales job, and this one particular psychiatrist spoke about bipolar disorder and integrating some innovative methods to treat it. I was ready for a change because I had been on the same medications, lithium and Tegretol, for sixteen and ten years, respectively. The opportunity to change up these medications and not just add on another medication was appealing for many reasons. Both medications can cause weight gain and fatigue, and they have also been linked to causing cognitive difficulties, such as thinking, reasoning, remembering, or learning. In addition to these side effects, the lithium caused cystic acne (mainly on my neck) that was both painful and what I called unattractive, although others told me they did not notice it.

My curiosity about new methods to treat bipolar disorder was heightened when listening to this psychiatrist speak. I had often thought there must be something new out there and that this doctor just might be the person for whom I was searching. I also wondered if lithium was really effective for me anymore, both because I had been on it for so many years (and taken off it once), and also because my levels were below the therapeutic range (although some people respond to less than the therapeutic level indicated).

I quickly scheduled an appointment for a consultation with this psychiatrist. I felt that we had a good connection and that he truly understood me. I agreed to take him on as my psychiatrist because he certainly sounded like he had some great ideas to tailor to my needs. He said he was very anxious to help me, and it would also be an interesting situation considering I would be a patient and would maintain a professional relationship with him.

When I came to him, it was the fall, and he noted my symptoms of seasonal affective disorder (SAD), which helped to explain the pattern of depressive symptoms I had experienced for years once the daylight hours began to shorten each fall. He recommended light therapy, and I started it immediately.

After our initial session, I shared with him that I was a bit hesitant about making any serious changes right away, because I was getting ready to move, which was a stressful time. Early in my diagnosis I had been cautioned that it was best not to make any major changes or disruptions, medication-wise, while going through stressful situations, and that had always made total sense to me. However, the psychiatrist thought this would be the best time to make some rather significant changes, so once again I trusted the doctor because he was a psychiatrist and that's what I was supposed to do. From what I had heard, he was well respected, and that gave me faith in him from the beginning.

Against what my gut was telling me, I went along with his new treatment plan, and I agreed to be taken off the lithium over a very short period of time (about a week) while remaining on Tegretol. He immediately added Risperdal, an antipsychotic medication approved for schizophrenia, but it was also known to help mania associated with bipolar disorder with fewer side effects than lithium—so he said. The side effects of Risperdal, as I later read in the prescribing information, included weight gain, insomnia, mild restlessness, drowsiness, and tremors, to name a few. To my dismay, soon after making these medication changes, I gradually began to slip into a very deep, dark, immobilizing depression. Aside from the beginning symptoms of SAD, which were mild at this time, I was not clinically depressed when I walked into his office for our initial consultation. I was functioning just fine and was simply looking for something to improve my quality of life by minimizing the negative side effects of the medications I was taking.

The depression started gradually, although I was not initially aware. I slowly lost patience for little things. Before I knew it, I could not handle anything without being completely overwhelmed; I simply could not cope. Focusing on waking up and getting out of bed without mulling over worries of what I would and would not be able to accomplish during the day was very difficult. Preparing for my daily calls for work and just getting out the door added to the stress I was already experiencing. Then there was the bulk of my job, which was calling on physicians in their offices. I did my best to keep a smile on my face and to be on top of my game throughout the sales part of the day. In addition to that, merely sitting at my desk at home and looking at bills to pay was enough to overtax my brain's ability to function.

Within two weeks I went from slowly crumbling with diminishing coping skills to what I refer to as my breakdown. Although I had experienced sixteen years of bipolar disorder, worked in a job where my primary product was an antidepressant (Wellbutrin SR), and called on psychiatrists, nothing prepared me for this sort of a depression. I had never experienced such engulfing confusion combined with an inability to process information and function. While in my new apartment one evening, I began to cry, sob, and rock. I was terrified of being alone in my new place. (How ironic after all I wanted was to have my own place.) I could see no end in sight and did not know what to do—except to get to a doctor. I was vulnerable and therefore dependent on my psychiatrist; he was my only hope, which was quite minimal at the time. Fortunately I still had the know-how to have him paged. I had him paged multiple times that day (a Saturday) with no response. I felt this was a true emergency and did not know what to do. I would never consider paging a doctor unless I thought it was totally necessary. By that evening he still had not called back, and I did not want to be alone, yet I did not know where to turn. I knew I could have gone to my brother's, but somehow that did not seem to be what I needed, and the thought of driving all the way to Gainesville, Virginia (which was forty-five minutes away) was not at all appealing to me. It was just too far to go, and I was not sure I could physically or mentally make that drive.

I ended up calling a friend in nearby DC who I felt would understand this situation, because he had a close family member who also had bipolar disorder. Up to the moment of calling him for help, I had not shared that part of my life with him; until then, it was something I wanted to keep to myself. He invited me over for a couple of hours—thank God for that—and got me through that extremely difficult evening. I was so relieved to feel safe, and he provided comfort and the moral support I sought without judgment. I still credit him to this day for saving me. I don't know if he ever really understood what he had done for me. I felt comforted and safe, and those two things seemed very necessary at that time.

After leaving his place that night, I recall getting terribly lost. Driving around and around was very scary, and not knowing where I was and the possible chance of not getting out of the city or getting home was overwhelming. Obviously my confusion had started to take over. I was familiar with confusion as one of the many possible symptoms of mania, but now it was also showing up in the depressive phase of the illness.

I paged my psychiatrist again on Sunday. He finally called me on Sunday evening. The first thing he said to me was, "You'll never believe where I am and who I'm with—I'm at the Redskins game with your boss!" (His first commitment to me was clearly as my doctor, but because he was at a pharmaceutical function with my manager, perhaps this is what was initially on his mind and why he responded that way.) I could have cared less where he was, and his comment was inappropriate. I felt like I was going to die or something close to that, and he was starting off his return call to me with that insignificant information. He said he did not realize something was *really* wrong. "Did you think I would page you five times, starting yesterday, if there wasn't something wrong?"

So, as could be expected, after he realized the severity of my problem, he saw me the next day for an emergency appointment. I have no idea how I was able to drive to the doctor's office. Upon arriving, I sat down and stared off blankly with no emotion to what was going on around me, wrapped up in my current state. I felt pathetic, and this type of emotional response was foreign to me. As I walked into his office, I saw a look of anguish in his eyes. He felt terrible. At first he considered hospitalizing me. The thought of having someone take over and take it all away was appealing, but my next thoughts were of what the aftereffects of hospitalization would mean to me and the length of time it would take to recover after returning to the real world.

Because there was not a concern for me doing harm to myself or others, the doctor and I agreed to alter my medications and make some lifestyle modifications to try to keep me out of the hospital. Medication changes meant immediately getting me off that Risperdal and back on lithium and incorporating the lifestyle modifications we had discussed earlier, including light therapy (both artificial and actual sunlight), exercise, and putting structure into the day so I would feel some sort of purpose and be less inclined to sleep. In particular, he recommended exercising outdoors in the sunlight for approximately thirty minutes to an hour as often as I could. This seemed to be nearly impossible at the time; the best I could start with was a ten-minute walk. It was in the fall when the weather was getting cooler, and even getting dressed to go outside was a struggle. I was very alone but felt I needed to be alone. I felt I needed to go through this and fix it all on my own because I believed it was some sort of self-induced sentence—more like a way of punishing myself for trying to seek out better treatment. Somewhere deep inside me, I knew I cared about getting well again; I just could not reach it. The depression was so overwhelming and consuming, and it had an extremely powerful hold on my ability to see a way out. Depression obscured my sense of hope.

The doctor also gave me his direct cell phone number for future emergencies of this nature, so that I would be assured of getting in touch with him. Giving out personal cell phone numbers had never been part of a psychiatric relationship for me. Even with the patient-professional confusion, I was still pretty shocked he would give me his personal cell number. It did give me some comfort, and I felt he trusted I would not abuse it.

I could not do anything for days—literally anything but get up to go to the bathroom. I did not eat for an entire week. I could not even get myself to move from the bed to the couch. Nothing interested me. Reaching over to pick up and read a book required too much effort, and even if I could get myself to pick it up, I would have not been able to focus.

Another thing that was remarkable (and new to me) about this episode of depression was that I did not want to talk to many people. I did not think anyone could help how I was feeling, and I did not want to burden anyone with my issues. I really thought I needed to take care of this myself, and by not mentioning it to others, the whole situation would be a lot easier. I did not even tell close friends who lived out of town, and to me that should have been easier than sharing with people who were in close proximity day to day. It was typical to go through periods of not talking to my friends out of town, so I just ignored everyone, with the exception of a friend from Pittsburgh who had also experienced depression. I called some other friends from Pittsburgh as time went on, but most did not really understand. They were, however, still able to lend support. Not sharing with others was entirely out of character for me. I had been blessed with so many wonderful and close friends, and I was normally very open with them. During this time, I talked mostly to my parents and my sister Debbie.

This first episode of depression forced me to go on short-term disability for three weeks, and I then worked another three weeks of half days. Fortunately I had a compassionate manager who respected the severity of the depression. According to company policy, I did not have to tell my manager anything; everything was kept confidential, and a communication was sent to the manager making him aware I was on leave. However, I felt the relationship I had with my manager was too strong not to tell him. Even with the difficulties I was experiencing in this depression, three full weeks still seemed like an excessive amount of time to be away from work, and I felt I was disappointing my boss and coworkers. I also felt it was a sign of weakness. Once my three weeks of half days were complete, I had ten consecutive days off due to holiday shutdown. The timing of the holiday shutdown proved to be beneficial for me so that I could prepare for full-time work in the new year, 2001.

I had always felt a weakness with my illness in whatever form it has taken, and not being able to function with the depression was an awful thing with which to come to terms. When I was manic, I felt so different, and at first my conscience did not get the best of me; it was the aftermath of picking up the pieces where I felt I had to take the responsibility for my actions. I was too hard on myself, as I often am. Clinical depression ran in a totally different order of emotions, where guilt of not being able to be productive rose into the middle of the episode. For me, I felt like I should be able to think clearly and be functional. Being incapacitated to such a degree felt very close to despair. I also had to come to terms with an entirely different kind of guilt—a feeling that I did this to myself by trying to improve my life. It was hard to admit that this illness (and my actions) had caused me to go on medical leave from my job. I had never even considered the possibility that I might have a debilitating depression; it took me some time to truly wrap my arms around that one.

Having the opportunity to reflect, I realized the duration of time off could have been worse. As I have been reminded by so many people, the most important thing was to take care of myself. I was certainly very fortunate to receive short-term disability leave with the depression after only working for this company for seven months. Far too many with mental illness are terminated for less. What was also helpful for me throughout this episode of depression was a strong support system from family, friends, and work, which made things a lot better. Later I came around to accepting that taking time off from work was really the only viable option available.

This scenario certainly scared me from making medication changes in the future and being able to truly trust another doctor, as I had done in the past. After several weeks with more medication on board, I did slowly recover. I went back to work, and let me tell you, although my self-esteem was getting better, I was not actually sure if I wanted to continue this job, or what I was even capable of doing for that matter. Once again my manager came through for me and let me know just how much he believed in me. That was right when I was returning to work, and he truly made a difference. I was able to slowly get back in the swing of things. Following the severity of this depression, it took a full six months to return back to my normal self. This was a major setback in my life and was all too consuming. The aftermath of the depression seemed to take longer than the manias.

After many visits to my psychiatrist, he actually apologized for his part in my temporary setback. All along I did feel his compassion for the situation; for him to actually accept accountability meant a lot to me. After all was said and done with this episode, I guess what I learned was that I was pretty good just how I was. Further, I did gain the insight I had been wondering about for so long: according to my doctor, I was a true lithium responder, and not only had it helped me with the highs many years ago, but it also clearly had antidepressant effects for me. I would never have found that out without this unfortunate experience.

Even though he seemed confident with his conclusion, there was one other possibility: we really didn't know what the outcome would have been had he taken me off lithium more gradually. After a person's brain is used to a medication and the brain chemistry has adapted for so many years, taking a patient off so abruptly could result in a very intense reaction. Either way, I realized that in order to move forward, I would have to accept that this happened, and there was no use going back to the past; it could not be changed. Some time needed to pass for me to get over the idea of what this one episode ultimately did to my life.

Probably the worst part of this new experience for me had to do with the future. I had not even considered that from this point forward, this newfound depression was going to be an ongoing occurrence. Originally I thought this severe clinical depression was an isolated incident, and it was over in my mind. However, what I did not realize was that Pandora's box had officially been opened, and my life would be altered forever. I had just wanted to tweak my medication to improve my quality of life, but somehow I ended up with the exact opposite of what I was searching for. Unfortunately, this was only the beginning of the storm that was brewing inside my head, and it would quickly impact almost every aspect of my life. Whereas the manic aspect of my bipolar disorder was manageable, it was now the depression that felt like the rug being pulled out from under me. Once again I was in a state of confusion, and I would again need to go through a rebuilding process.

Throughout that year I was introduced to milder forms of depression, where my medication had to be modified to help prevent me from moving into another major lapse. I don't recall having these types of depressions prior to 2000. I was now on lithium, Tegretol, Wellbutrin SR, and Zoloft. Although I was afraid to take the Wellbutrin again, this time it was the sustained release formulation, and I responded to it just fine, without the side effects from the immediate release formulation. I continued to have trouble focusing, so my psychiatrist tried putting me on *five* different stimulants. Unfortunately they all were too activating and made me so edgy that I had to discontinue each one.

Most of the milder clinical depressions were undetectable to those around me, but sometimes I just could not put on a happy face. When I felt this way, I had a very difficult time faking things, and when it got too bad, it was noticeable to some people I knew well. The symptoms of the milder depressions were not severe enough to take time off work, other than a couple days here and there, but they did induce a lack of self-esteem and feelings of inadequacy, even when others (including my manager) thought I was doing just fine. I continued to experience feelings of guilt that I was not giving the job 100 percent effort, because of how hard I needed to push myself to get up in the morning. I typically made it through the day, although it was much more of a struggle and took all I had just to complete my work. Getting back home was something I really looked forward to because I was both physically and emotionally drained by the end of each day. I became increasingly critical of and hard on myself, and the depression made me feel that I was not functioning as well as I probably was. I have a very strong work ethic, instilled in me from my father, and the feeling that I was not performing up to my own standards was both aggravating and troublesome.

Aside from that, there were increased amounts of psychiatrist visits, adjustments to my medication, and so forth. I never dreamed I would be spending so much time at the doctor's office again, not to mention any financial aspect involved—the insurance company made so many errors, and when I was not feeling well, this made things much more difficult. I'm not fully convinced all the appointments were necessary, and it is hard to believe that just several years prior, my psychiatric visits were once a year.

Successive depressions can require less of a stressor to trigger the onset of another episode. Those stressors can range anywhere from something severe to something fairly benign. Examples of stressors include situational factors (stress, overcommitting, an unexpected event that changes up daily routine, and family factors like anger or irritability over a misunderstanding or concern about illnesses of loved ones), seasonal changes, and even medication changes. Sometimes there is no stressor at all.

Throughout these ongoing depressions, my job satisfaction and confidence in my ability to perform my tasks continued to be a constant frustration. My psychiatrist's observation was that when I began to become depressed, I lost my self-assurance, and the first symptom of my depression was disinterest in my job. After he brought this to my attention, I felt it resonated with me and realized just how many times that happened: as the depression began to occur and then subside, my job satisfaction and overall confidence level oscillated from struggling with it immensely to being okay. I also did not have the self-confidence level or the energy I needed to pursue another career path, so I stayed where I felt safe.

A possible medication-induced trigger for one of my depressions was the medication I took for the cystic acne, Accutane. Over the past decade I had had two treatments of Accutane with no side effects of which I was aware. In the summer of 2001, my acne had flared up again. While calling on a customer who was a dermatologist, he saw the cystic acne on my neck and immediately recognized it was a side effect of lithium; he suggested I start another course of Accutane, knowing I had been on it two times prior. I was on the Accutane this time for a period of approximately two months. During the initial stages of Accutane treatment, the symptoms of depression arose. Toward the end of the Accutane treatment, my psychiatrist informed me of the correlation between Accutane and depression. Under contraindications in the warnings section of Accutane's product information, it states under the heading of psychiatric disorders: "Accutane may cause depression, psychosis and, rarely, suicidal ideation, suicide attempts, suicide, and aggressive and/or violent behaviors."[1] Even with this new information I had learned, I felt completing the course of treatment would be better than stopping so close to the end. For me, the benefit of eliminating and preventing further cystic acne outweighed the risk of depression at this stage of treatment. I thought I could hold out for just a few more weeks.

The causal relationship between Accutane and depression for me had been suggested, but not confirmed, because there were too many factors involved to determine if this was the sole cause. My psychiatrist, not my dermatologist, told me about this correlation. Considering the dermatologist immediately recognized the root cause of my cystic acne was a direct result of lithium, it would be a fair deduction on his part to know that lithium was the primary treatment for bipolar disorder. I strongly believe it is the prescribing doctor's responsibility to be aware of any side effects and to share this awareness with the patient receiving treatment so that an informed decision can be made before starting treatment. And yes, even though this information is found in the prescribing information, there is so much information on there that it is difficult to decipher it all. As consumers we are often encouraged *not* to read the whole prescribing information insert, otherwise we will think we are experiencing every adverse side effect listed. This is not to take the responsibility off ourselves to be informed, however it is disconcerting that the physician would rely solely on the patient reading the prescribing information for something so severe as depression (knowing the patient has bipolar disorder).

Historically for me, after taking Accutane, the cystic acne would go away for about six months to a year and then come back. It is possible that for me the acne was related to something hormonal, but ultimately it was most likely the lithium that caused or aggravated it. This issue is known for some patients on lithium, and unfortunately, either choice—going back on the Accutane or staying off it—had its downside. I came to the decision that once this course of treatment was up, I would not entertain going on Accutane again. I chose to deal with the possibility of the acne recurring in exchange for my mental stability. (I was told it would go away eventually, and for whatever reason, it never returned.)

To help avoid a seasonal depressive stressor in the fall of 2001, I began to resume my light therapy again. However, even after a week-long trip to Florida (in the sun) in October, as the days got shorter and the sunlight gradually diminished back in Washington, DC, the sensations of depression began to settle in. Once again I complained about my job becoming tougher, and my lack of interest in it was obvious to me and my family and friends. The correlation of not feeling well emotionally and work becoming more of a struggle was quite clear. Considering I was still not in a job that enabled me to do the social service–oriented work I desired, the depression (even if only the warning signs) exacerbated the feeling of a lack of sense of purpose.

My second major clinical depression occurred the following year, in September 2002. The fall season had arrived again, and I began to have a difficult time with my diminishing coping skills. I was successfully maintaining the healthy things I needed to do in order to stay as well as I could, yet I had begun to spiral down in spite of these efforts once again. I was compelled to go on medical leave a second time in the middle of September for three weeks. I remember struggling to decide whether or not to attend a week-long work trip in Florida. I really wanted to push forward and go (it was during the last of the weeks I was on medical leave), but in the end I just could not do it. Again, that lack of confidence had taken over, and I was afraid I was not ready.

After the three weeks were up, I returned to work for a week and then was off for another week of planned vacation. I continued to feel better as my medications were adjusted to the appropriate dosages. I worked hard at doing all the right things to support my progress. After several months I did feel like my old self again and had regained my confidence. Even so, this illness was wearing me down.

The beginning signs of my third major clinical depression came one year later, after the breakup of a serious relationship in August 2003. I was definitely a mess. This person I was in love with had walked out the door, and it was very painful. So many people kept asking about him, and I had to relive it over and over again. After weeks went on, the situational depression I was experiencing changed into a full-blown clinical depression—and it was the fall again. I did not think that this illness would come to consume my life yet again. Although it was very difficult and the feelings were very similar to what I had felt in my previous depressions (including my coping skills weakening and my self-esteem fading away), this time I was able to regain my balance without taking medical leave from work. I still struggled with work but required only a few days off. The main factors involved with this recovery were the changes to my medication and taking a brief time-out. One of the reasons this successive depression was so upsetting was because, up until this point, I had made so many positive steps in learning how to deal with my illness and warding it off, and it did not seem fair to have it happen again.

During this third depression, while still under the care of my psychiatrist, he prescribed Zoloft for me once again. I had been on and off Zoloft during my time of treatment with him. This time I experienced side effects from the Zoloft: constant nausea in addition to anxiety one hour after taking my medication. He told me to take some Zantac for the nausea. The last thing I wanted to do was take *another* pill to combat the side effects of *another* medication, and the anxiety was still not taken into account. My psychiatrist was under the impression that the Zoloft was not the source of the anxiety. I wanted to be off the Zoloft, but I wanted to wait until I was given the green light.

Within several weeks the side effects of nausea and anxiety were too much. I quit taking the Zoloft cold turkey, without the psychiatrist's consent, knowing I was taking a risk for the depression to not get better, but I kept in mind that I had only been on it a few weeks. I want to be clear that not checking in with the prescribing physician before altering any medication being taken is never recommended. For me, at this juncture I had reached my personal limit, and enough was enough: experiencing nausea and anxiety in exchange for alleviating the depression was a deal I was unwilling to accept. I was not ceasing all medications; I was still on two potent mood stabilizers. I made the decision not to put my faith in a pill, but to put it in myself to make the commitment to do whatever it would take for me to minimize the depression on my own, through proper sleep, exercise, diet, and light therapy. I felt I knew myself and how my body responded well enough to make this choice, in order to achieve symptom alleviation.

The nausea and anxiety subsided almost immediately after stopping the Zoloft and getting it out of my system. While I was doing all I knew to take the best care of myself for the depression response, my psychiatrist continued to insist that the anxiety was not the result of the Zoloft and that I needed to continue the Zoloft to help against that very same anxiety. This experience gave me the final push to consult with a new psychiatrist, because the one I was seeing failed to acknowledge all of my concerns with medication and my well-being. Only weeks prior I had been presented with an opportunity to meet with a new psychiatrist, and I waited with great anticipation for this transition to occur. I felt that finding someone new was long overdue.

Up to the point of experiencing my first clinical depression, I was taking life as it came and doing just fine maintaining a sense of normalcy. The illness was not me, but a part of me—and a manageable one at that. When I am doing well, it is incredibly difficult to believe that this other side of me even exists. Experiencing clinical depression goes against who I feel I am. Dwelling on guilty feelings about what I have not accomplished and cannot do are predominant in the midst of the depression. Self-blame also contributes to a slower progression in getting well, slowing down the healing process. Many people who experience clinical depression cannot get it in their minds that it is not their fault. At this time I was new to it all and was learning how to deal with it in a way that I could try to control. Similar to when the manic symptoms were present, I wanted to be as in control of the depressive aspect of this illness as I could, so that I could get back to living again without living the illness all the time.

Chapter 8
Beyond the Consultation: Psychiatry and Competent Treatment

OVER THE YEARS I have been in treatment for bipolar disorder, I have seen a variety of psychiatrists and several therapists. I can recall nineteen actual psychiatrists, but there could have been more. Throughout my treatment, I have learned how important it is to receive competent treatment.

Psychiatrists and therapists actually have a lot of power and even some control over their patients. When they build and hopefully gain trust, their role continues to become increasingly important. Putting our lives into another's hands can be both frightening and unsettling. After all, they are treating a part of us that controls our thinking and emotions. When prescribing medication that affects brain chemistry, emotional well-being must be closely monitored and evaluated to ensure the best treatment possible. Of course this is not to say that the responsibility for the patient's mental health outcome lies solely with the treating physician. However, he or she does play an integral role in the overall wellness of the patient, as the patient's thoughts and behaviors impact all aspects of daily life.

During my first hospitalization, I came to understand the importance of competent treatment from psychiatrists, nurses, and administrative personnel. One of the first psychiatrists to play a very important role in my recovery was Dr. Gleditsch, who was my psychiatrist while in the hospital. I know he truly cared about me and did everything in his power to make me comfortable in my surroundings. There was also a kind nurse who had a very nurturing demeanor. She gave me some good advice and was very understanding. I still remember exactly where she was standing in front of the nurses' station when she shared the following thoughts with me. "Life will tend to be overwhelming at times. There are always many things going on at the same time. It is important to concentrate on one small thing at a time instead of looking at life as one huge problem." That advice is still very valuable to me and has helped me when I start too many projects at a time. Also, I was very fortunate to have one other hospital employee from whom I could seek support. She was the head of the nursing staff and, coincidentally, also a member of our church. Whenever I had a problem, I could go to her for help, and she was there for me. Her ability to quickly troubleshoot a potential problem before it escalated was extremely helpful, and it showed me how great it was having people on the "inside" on your side.

Unfortunately, this is when I also learned about the hindrances of less than optimal care. At this point in time, the only people I and the other patients ever had any issues with were a few of the nurses. Some clearly should not have been in this profession. Luckily we patients had each other to fall back on.

The four hospital stays I had probably saved my life—especially the first three. Competent and thorough mental health treatment is a huge concern of mine for people today, specifically in regard to insurance companies. Today, insurances do not pay for the length of days I had, and I truly do not know what the outcome would have been for me if I were experiencing all I did for the first time in today's world. Although I certainly realize there are times when spending too much time in the hospital can have negative effects on the patient, there are also certainly many times when one clearly needs more help. I do think there are a number of people who need more than a just a few days in the hospital—especially when it is their first experience with the illness. It also depends on the severity of the depressive or manic episode at the time or the state of vulnerability of the patient. This is not a "one size fits all" situation.

Given today's advancements in medicine, patients are often discharged and sent out the door to continue recovery on their own, even though they may not feel capable. If the person is not able to take on the responsibility for himself or herself, this responsibility will often fall to a family member, a caregiver, a friend … or no one at all. Some psychiatrists require that a family member or close friend accompany the patient to the initial appointment to ensure he or she is providing accurate symptomatology and details to ensure the doctor gets a clear picture of where the patient stands with their illness. For me, I had my family to watch over me while I was in this situation. Thank God I had the help that I did.

Even with all my experience and information about my illness, I have not always been capable of doing what I need to do just to get by. My concerns are for those who have not yet been diagnosed properly or at all, or who have been diagnosed but lack the tools to gain insight into their bipolar disorder. It is no wonder to me why there are so many people with mental illness who are homeless, in jail, or unemployed, when they cannot receive the help they require. I can't imagine how many people with mental illness are surviving out there on their own.

When I was first diagnosed in 1984, the role of the psychiatrist was not only for medication monitoring, but just as important, it also involved intensive psychotherapy. My appointments typically ranged anywhere from thirty to sixty minutes. For me, it would be rare to have an appointment lasting fifteen minutes or less.

Over time I have witnessed a shift in the role of psychiatrists. Largely due to the influx of managed care insurance and general increased costs, many psychiatrists are found to be in a difficult position where they often cannot maintain their practices by practicing therapy as well as medication maintenance. In the case where a psychiatrist primarily manages the medication maintenance, the patients are referred out for separate therapy. Psychiatric visits are then often limited to medication management appointments typically lasting fifteen minutes.

Each psychiatrist chooses to practice in his or her own way. Some psychiatrists continue to conduct therapy for various reasons, including maintaining the continuity of therapeutic care due to potential communication lapses when the patient requires two mental health providers (separate psychiatrist and therapist). Because of current third-party payment systems, insurance companies decide what is covered and what is not, and mental health providers typically cannot bill for talking to one another about their common patient. Therefore less communication between therapists and psychiatrists occurs, leaving a gap in therapeutic care.

When a person with a mental illness is seeking out a new psychiatrist or therapist for the first time—including due to an insurance change or a move—the process can be very challenging. Many scenarios can occur and many factors fluctuate. As the patient begins, he may be anywhere in the range from a stable state of mind to being in a completely overwhelmed state of distress. Where he is emotionally also dictates the ease or difficulty of taking the next steps. Sometimes someone else notices something is not quite right with his behavior and sets up an appointment for him via a doctor or hospital.

If you are on your own, the process of finding the best mental healthcare professional for your needs usually proceeds in a manner similar to these steps.

- The patient admits there is a problem that he cannot resolve on his own.

- The patient sees a primary care provider (PCP) first and asks what to do.

- The PCP will hopefully refer him to psychiatrist or therapist depending on need.

- PCPs may be forced to treat the patient due to lack of available mental healthcare providers (and they are not extensively trained to do so).

- The patient calls the insurance company for a list of providers (if they have insurance and the insurance company actually has a list). The patient then is usually referred within his insurance plan to a mental health division.

Calling from a list of providers within an insurance carrier is not as straightforward as it may seem due to several variables.

- The nonavailability of one or more of the psychiatrists or therapists on the list (for example, many may not be accepting new patients, or their next available appointment for a new patient is too long to wait; often this wait time can be over three months).

- With each phone call the patient experiences the frustration and emotional drain of having to repeat the reasons for calling.

- Once the patient finally secures an appointment, then there are payment issues with which to contend.

Larger and larger numbers of providers are now requiring patients to process the claims themselves. This growing trend started in the midnineties. While one can appreciate that psychiatrists and therapists cannot provide their highest level of care with the additional hours it takes to complete insurance paperwork, this creates a potential burden or barrier for the patient to obtain reimbursement, again depending on where they are emotionally.

Once one gets past all that, then there is the chance of not connecting on a personal level with that healthcare professional. If this is the case, one must start all over again from the beginning. To the patient, an hour's worth of pouring out one's personal life story is emotionally exhaustive, and this may prohibit the patient from beginning the process all over again; a patient may either stay with the provider who is not a good fit or even give it up altogether.

Over the years in my dealings with this illness, I have had to build many different relationships with numerous doctors and therapists. Having to get to know and trust so many people does not come easy for many, but for me, I felt there really was not a choice. I certainly choose to be under a psychiatrist's care versus not being under one at all. Throughout the years of my hospitalizations (1984–1990), the amount of times I would see my psychiatrist fluctuated. During a difficult time it might be once a week, and then as I would get better, the visits would become less frequent. Once stabilized, I saw my psychiatrist only once a year between 1992 and 1995; during this yearly appointment I also had my lithium and Tegretol medication blood levels drawn and measured. The yearly psychiatric appointment allowed fifty to sixty minutes to review the year. I was not receiving any type of additional therapy during these three years except at the end, when I sought out several sessions of therapy due to the breakup of a serious relationship.

When relocating from Pittsburgh to the Washington, DC, area in 1995, due to the protocol of my new HMO for my new job, I rotated through psychiatrists to whoever was available. Establishing a relationship with a psychiatric medical professional was difficult in this scenario because there was no continuity of care. (As fate would have it, nine years later I was reacquainted with a psychiatrist from this same HMO. He informed me that he left the HMO for this very reason.)

One particular psychiatrist at this HMO casually suggested I try therapy but did not offer any direction as to why she thought I needed therapeutic sessions. The idea sounded okay to me, so I agreed. Her referral was to a therapist who, after one session, realized I was doing well with my illness and did not have any stressors that warranted therapy. With nothing related to my illness to discuss, I suggested we talk about my current boyfriend and concerns I had about the relationship. After three total visits the therapist agreed that therapy was not a necessary tool for me. We concluded that I was managing the illness well and holding my own.

With new employment in 1999 came another new insurance provider, and thus a new psychiatrist. I was comforted by the stability provided by one psychiatrist as opposed to many. I saw him several times over the course of just over a year, and our sessions lasted for approximately thirty minutes. Additional therapy was not recommended.

In 2000, several months after starting with a different employer, I chose to see a new psychiatrist. When I asked about additional therapy, this particular psychiatrist actually advised me not to, because I had bipolar disorder, and it could be managed with medication. I stayed with this psychiatrist until the fall of 2003. Although I received what I felt was less than optimal treatment, I continued with this psychiatrist for three years. I had trusted him early on, and at times the thought of starting over again was too exhausting.

My third experience with therapy was initiated by me, not by a psychiatrist. It again was not centered on the illness, but on yet another relationship. In January 2003, while my boyfriend (who lived in Toronto) and I were on a break, I chose to see a relationship counselor to work on my concerns with the attachment issues he continued to have with his ex-wife, and to discover if I was responding in the healthiest manner to make our relationship work. I saw this counselor over the course of three months for a total of approximately eight sessions. During this experience I allowed myself to be convinced that it was me who had the issues with his ex-wife, and it was my nonacceptance of their ongoing codependency that added to our problems. I went so far as to write a letter to my boyfriend saying that I accepted everything and basically said that it was my problem and through therapy I was able to see that. I actually read that letter to my therapist. She thought it was great and encouraged me to send it.

In hindsight, I see that I allowed myself to be swayed by the opinion of a person with credentials. Her expertise in the relationship field led me to believe that my boyfriend's codependent relationship with his ex-wife was not only okay but also my responsibility to accept. What I learned from this experience was to pay attention to my own instincts and to understand that a therapist's word merits weight, but the responsibility for making a decision is mine. I really wanted to be convinced that what I knew could somehow be altered. I feel that because she told me what I wanted to hear, I did not listen to my gut. I share this because a therapist, even working with the best of intentions, is offering you the best of their expertise and experience, and depending on the therapist, the outcome may differ.

In September of that same year, I had an opportunity for a consultation with a new psychiatrist. I was hopeful, as I felt I was not receiving optimal care from my current psychiatrist. I had made it my goal to do everything in my power to keep healthy for the next few months while I was waiting for my consultation. This was my plan, anyway. Unfortunately I was forced to go back to see my current psychiatrist during my three-month waiting period, because I was experiencing depression again and needed some medication tweaking. I saw him a couple times in July, but then the visits increased in the month of August as I continued to struggle. I was ready to leave the provider from whom I was receiving treatment, and my hopes for the new consultation were very high.

When I went to my last appointment with the current psychiatrist, I was in such a down state that I had to take off work for several days. I could not function properly enough to work and felt a couple days off might help to prevent me from spiraling down any further. My confidence was going, and I was having difficulty coping—all the typical symptoms. After waiting almost two and a half hours (yes, that's right—there was always an hour minimum wait for this psychiatrist; maybe if he did not cram three patients into a fifteen-minute slot, that would not have happened), he basically told me that between the SAD, the breakup of a serious relationship, and the lack of Zoloft (which I went off in late spring), my brain just could not deal. His recommendation was to add another antidepressant, a selective serotonin reuptake inhibitor (SSRI). I resisted because of the side effects (especially with the Zoloft), and I did not want another SSRI on board or any other medication at all. His response was, "How about Lexapro? It does not have as much weight gain." My response to him was no, because Lexapro was also an SSRI and did have the weight gain side effect. This was well-known, and he knew that I knew about antidepressants because of my job. To someone who is naïve to medications, this might work, but with me it just did not fly. He asked, "Don't you want to get better?" Of course I did, but there must be another way. With that he increased my Wellbutrin SR to 400 mg and sent me on my way with a sample and a prescription for Lexapro. I did not fill that prescription because I knew I had the consultation with the new doctor later that week. If I could just hang in there until then, maybe I would get a different treatment plan.

Two days seemed like a very long wait, but my appointment finally arrived. Many emotions came out during this appointment. After reviewing my history and after speaking with me for an hour and a half, this new psychiatrist was sincerely concerned about the care I had been receiving over the past few years. He also wondered why I did not have psychotherapy, because it was often a part of his suggested treatment plan for his patients with bipolar disorder. My previous psychiatrist's view was that because my illness was biological, I did not need psychotherapy, whereas my view was that I may have benefited from it. My former psychiatrist's continual assurance of the biological etiology reiterated that the illness did not warrant it, and in the end I considered this to be okay because it meant less time for me to spend tending to my illness. I also liked the idea that he was validating I did not need therapy because bipolar disorder is not environmentally based.

The new psychiatrist also wondered why I stayed with my former psychiatrist after what had happened three years ago (taking me off the lithium that led to the depression and then the subsequent depressions), given my own personal knowledge about the illness. I told him I now realize that I felt a little like what some people feel when in an abusive relationship: he kind of had a hold on me and kept insisting that he was "helping me to get better," and therefore I kept coming back. Because my depression was rather cyclical, I felt that the doctor took pride in healing me, and when I would get sick again he would heal me again, over and over. I also developed a good doctor-patient relationship with him over time, he knew so much about me, and I just did not want to ruin all that we had built over these years. At one point when my insurance was changing, I told him I was going to leave, and he actually acted sincerely hurt and said he would work out something with my insurance to keep me. He did this, and I felt that was very nice for him to go above and beyond for me.

I now think there was something wrong with this psychiatric treatment approach. He truly was able to "keep" me, even when my inclinations were to seek out other treatment. He certainly knew how vulnerable his patients were given the very nature of mental illness, and I think it was quite peculiar that he behaved in such a manner. I do know that he seemed to feel responsible for me after what had happened after the first depression, when he took me off the lithium. From this experience I learned so much about human behavior from both sides of the chair. To me, the role of the psychiatrist is more than simply understanding the use of basic medications; it is also about putting the patient's care and well-being before one's own need to heal someone. Whether consciously or unconsciously, the concept of "first do no harm" seemed to get lost along the way of my treatment.

Although I was happy and grateful to have had the new consultation, I could not help but be disappointed when he informed me that his schedule did not afford him the time to see me as his patient. He agreed to refer me to someone he trusted to give me the proper care I required, so I was appreciative of that.

As upset as I was regarding the care I had received over the past three years, I also had some newfound hope for the future. As I left his office, I felt this was the beginning of the rest of my life. I also needed to get in touch with my former psychiatrist, to let him know I would be leaving him. I was not quite sure of the appropriate way to handle this, but I knew it would not be face-to-face. I left a message with the office manager letting the doctor know I had had a consultation with a new psychiatrist, and he was going to refer me out. The office manager questioned why I was leaving, and I told her I felt I was not receiving appropriate care. She said she would leave the doctor a message, and she was sure that he would want to talk to me via phone about it. I never heard from him. After three years of treatment, I was a little surprised I did not even get a return phone call.

Immediately after the initial consultation, I sensed I needed help soon because I was going through a depression at that time and was very anxious to get started. I did not hear from the new psychiatrist's office for days and was getting more frustrated by this; my depression was worsening. After two weeks I got the answer I was hoping for. The answer was somehow what I had a feeling it would be: his assistant relayed to me that the doctor could not find a psychiatrist in the area who could take on a new patient whom he could trust with my situation. He said that because of my treatment over the past few years, he did not want just anybody to treat me … so he decided to take me on as his patient. I had really hoped this would happen. It was truly a blessing and something I appreciated immensely.

At my next appointment with him in November, he made some minor adjustments in my medication. He first slightly decreased the amount of lithium (900 mg to 750 mg), but he instructed me to take the full dose before bed instead of in divided doses in the morning and evening. He made the same adjustment with the Carbetrol (extended released Tegretol), although the dosage remained the same at 400 mg. The divided dosage of Wellbutrin SR (150 mg in the morning and night) was given as a total dose of 300 mg in the morning. All these modifications were to optimize the effects of these medications at their specific times (i.e., the more sedating medications would have their effect while I slept, and the energizing effect of Wellbutrin SR would help me during the day).

The doctor and I also discussed my anxiety-like symptoms as well as what I described as an "out of it" feeling I had been experiencing for several years. For the "out of it" feeling, he desired to get a more specific understanding of my symptoms. It was difficult to put into words, but the main sensations were feeling spacey and out of sorts. He came to the conclusion that the combination of Wellbutrin SR and lithium were creating these side effects. To counter these undesired reactions, he added 10 mg of Propranalol (a blood pressure medication, but a very small dosage) to my treatment regimen. This small dosage is often taken for stage fright, therefore abating the side effects that mimicked anxiety. I was in complete amazement when these sensations subsided, because I had felt them for a couple years and had described them to my former psychiatrist, who basically dismissed them. Losing that "out of it" feeling made me feel normal again.

He also had me increase my one tablet of Omega 3 (fish oil) to four capsules, and he prescribed .025 mcg of Synthroid to increase my T4 hormone level, to elevate my energy. These were all to be added to my regular supplement regimen of a multivitamin, calcium with magnesium and zinc, and vitamins C, E, and B complex that I was already taking.

After several days of these changes, one Sunday I suddenly became very disoriented. It started while shopping at a retail store while an assistant was helping me look for an item. I quickly had to get out of the store. I next went to the grocery store, where the disorientation hit me a lot harder. I knew where I was but felt totally out of it. I made it out of the store and back in my car, and I called my good friend Sherri in Kansas. She said it sounded as if I had just woken up. After explaining what was going on, I told her I felt as if my speech was delayed. She said that was probably because it *was* delayed. I was very scared and got home as quickly as I could. I wanted to call the doctor but only had his phone number at George Washington University, where his research and academic position was located at the time. I knew I would have to wait until Monday.

This pretty much messed up the rest of my evening, and I was scared wondering what change in my new treatment plan could be affecting me this way. I called in sick Monday because I knew I could not function in a proper manner. I was able to reach the psychiatrist's office first thing in the morning, and his assistant gave me his home office phone number. I left him a detailed message, and he called back shortly after. He told me to stop taking the fish oil right away (unfortunately I had already taken three capsules Sunday night and one that morning—I had no idea what was causing this to go on). He also asked me why I did not try him over the weekend, and he sounded surprised when I told him I did not have his home office number. I suppose it was just an oversight; he had assumed I had it. Getting a phone number for emergencies is one of the many important things to find out when starting with a new psychiatrist. This was something I was not thinking about because I was not anticipating any strange things to happen.

I continued throughout the week with only one Omega 3 capsule and had different moments of feeling out of it, but they were not as severe as Sunday. I tried to stay positive and kept thinking that it was going to get better at some point soon. The disorientation subsided with the lower dose of Omega 3. The actual depression felt much better; I was now on the right combination of meds and experienced a minimization of the previous negative side effects.

I had faithfully used the light therapy every morning since seeing the new psychiatrist. He and I were sure that it had an effect on the way I was feeling. Although I did fill the prescription for Synthroid, I shared my concerns with the doctor after learning more about thyroid function and how the Synthroid (T4) converts to T3 in the body. I had tried numerous other medications that stimulated T3 levels during treatment with my first depression, and each made me feel very edgy and like I was going to jump out of my skin. I was afraid of a similar reaction with the Synthroid and was therefore hesitant to take it. In the end, we decided I would not start it. My goal, as I reminded him, was to be on as few medications as possible while remaining well.

A month into treatment, he recommended psychotherapy in addition to our psychiatric visits, to deal with some of my current stressful life situations with which I was struggling. I agreed because I wanted to achieve overall wellness; with wellness, I would ultimately be able to pursue the goals I wanted to obtain in my life.

He suggested cognitive-behavioral therapy, which focuses in part on current behavioral patterns and restructuring priorities and goals in order to achieve them. Other forms of therapy, such as analytic therapy, would have me analyzing my past, and this would not address my current problems. I took his advice. After seeing one therapist, she suggested I see an additional one so I would have some sort of basis to determine with whom I might be most comfortable. I thought this was kind of odd because it was not my intention to seek out another therapist after meeting with her; I thought she would probably work out fine. The thought of sharing my whole story again was not appealing to me, either. However, this ended up being a very good suggestion on her part. I sought out another therapist with whom I *really* connected. This new therapist ended up being fantastic for me, and I remained with him for about six months.

The therapist and I started with my background and quickly established my three key issues to address: number one was the relationship with my boyfriend; two, my job; and three, to buy or not to buy my apartment that was being converted into a condominium. Because of the therapist's insightfulness, he recognized my need for structure to achieve goals, just like I had incorporated structure into my daily routine. He gave me an assignment right away to set goals for a timeline of when I wanted to have these issues resolved and what I wanted for my life.

The easiest issue was my condo. However, it really was not that easy for me—I thought about it and checked out so many things before I was truly ready. I had been given sixty days to make a decision, and that did not seem like a lot of time. However, I was soon able to recognize that buying the condo proved to be the best decision: it was a good investment, and it also removed the stress of needing to move.

Dealing with my overall lack of job satisfaction would be an ongoing process. I did not feel I was being challenged enough in my pharmaceutical sales position to make enough of a purposeful difference, and I desired to achieve a bigger impact regarding mental health issues.

Revising my resume was something that had been hanging over my head for some time, yet it was something I wanted to complete. My therapist gave me suggestions of where to go to get help with my resume, and before I knew it, that thing that was so difficult for me to do was done. That was a good start for the job search. After doing some research on other professions, I did not find anything worth leaving my current position for, and I decided to stay.

Last but not least was the issue that would demand the most emotional work, and that was to get some resolution to this relationship that had gone on (and off) with my boyfriend for almost two years. Both my therapist and I knew that resolving the relationship issue one way or another was essential for me to move forward with my life. He knew the relationship was causing too much pain for me, and this back-and-forth stuff was ridiculous. He also knew how much we loved each other and thought we needed to be in the same city to really know if it could work.

Together, the therapist and I created a possible solution: I would temporarily relocate to Toronto for a couple months. This would mean quitting my job, getting my own place, and figuring out how to occupy my free time by volunteering or something similar. I knew that this relationship was important to pursue in the same city. I presented the option to my boyfriend, but in the end he said no. Giving him this choice to make was one of the best things I could have done.

He wanted to maintain a friendship, but it was now time for me to let him go—completely. I had already said good-bye to him so many times before, and this time it was not so bad. I did not slide down into a depression as a result of it; in fact, I got stronger and felt empowered.

For me, therapy helped me to see what the real issues were that were guiding my life in positive and negative ways, and to put me on a structured path to resolve the obstacles that were currently in my way. I felt that this type of therapy worked for me. My therapist's encouragement to set these goals was imperative to keep me moving. I left therapy after about six months when my immediate problems were resolved. We never worked on any issues that were related directly to (or were a result of) my bipolar disorder, which seemed to be the pattern with me and therapy.

I contacted my psychiatrist in August the following year when I first felt signs of the depression coming on, so that we could plan out a strategy to minimize the symptoms. With the days getting shorter again, life was beginning to get more difficult as the precursors of my depression started to present themselves. For the next two months I saw him approximately every ten days. He introduced Lamictal (an antiseizure medication also indicated for bipolar depression) to my regimen in the beginning of September. Over the course of the next four months, we slowly titrated up until we achieved an optimal dose. With all my efforts to live a healthy life, in addition to my continued spiritual growth earlier in the year, I thought that it would be easier this time around and that I would be able avoid the seasonal depression. I knew if I could just make it until October, I would be okay. In October I would be off work for an entire month and would travel to Florida to spend quality time with my grandfather. Although the original plan for the trip was not to relieve my depression, the timing ended up being perfect.

I made it through and was off to Florida on October 1, 2004. Not only did I get quality time with my grandfather, but also my stress level was very minimal, and I got to be in the sunshine by both the pool and the beach. There was also the peaceful, cumulative effect of going to the beach at night for sunset.

Having a competent doctor has made all the difference in the world for me. Even so, life with bipolar disorder will never be totally normal. Although I have led a very productive and happy life, it is so important to know that this illness is never completely going away, and acknowledging that is very important. I may appear on the outside to be just fine, but I still deal with side effects from medications that can affect my everyday responsibilities. Sometimes I feel out of it, sometimes I'm a little shaky, and sometimes not feeling well is part of this illness for me. At times (especially during my golden years) the illness seems like it does not even exist, but there is a constant daily reminder when I take my medication; seeing a psychiatrist on a somewhat regular basis confirms it as well.

Because I am now more aware of the warning signs of getting sick (either manic or depressed), adhering to lifestyle modifications and working together with my psychiatrist (particularly a competent psychiatrist who understands the complexity of bipolar disorder), I now have the tools to manage my bipolar disorder, and I have been able to avoid the hospital for the last twenty years.

Chapter 9
Wanting the Pain to Go Away: Suicide

THE IDEA OF TAKING one's life is extremely difficult for anyone to understand, especially if one has not experienced clinical depression. Even though I have experienced severe ups and downs, I cannot fully comprehend the act of suicide. I have made much effort to try to understand, but I think only those who have undergone the contemplation, planning, and perhaps follow-through of the attempt may fully express all the personal components that formulate this particular path.

In addition to contemplation about suicide, there are three other terms used by professionals in any discussion about suicide: suicide ideation, suicide attempt, and suicide. Suicide ideation is the formulation of the idea or plan for the taking of one's own life. A suicide attempt is the following through with the plans to end one's life. Suicide is the successful attempt that ends in death. (Note: these are very general definitions.) The presence of one state of mind or action alone does not guarantee the surfacing of another; there are no absolutes linking these terms together. For example, suicidal thoughts themselves do not necessarily manifest to ideation, and suicide ideation does not mean an attempt will be made. A study released by the Substance Abuse and Mental Health Administration (SAMHSA) in September 2009 revealed that of the nearly 8.3 million US adults who had serious thoughts of committing suicide in the past year, 2.3 million made a plan, and 1.1 million actually made the attempt to commit suicide.[1]

Also, the absence of suicide ideation does not mean a suicide attempt will not be made. Suicide attempts sometimes occur without the person ever identifying with an ideation. Sometimes people deny suicide ideation because they are seriously planning to do it and don't want to alert a caregiver (doctor, family member, friend) who might prevent it. Unfortunately, any serious action taken to attempt suicide has no guaranteed outcome: some are found in the midst of the attempt or ask for medical intervention, but others tragically die.

As for myself, be it my faith, strong sense of hope, family upbringing, genetic makeup, family support and their lack of judgment, or possibly a little of all these combined, I have been very fortunate not to have experienced suicidal thoughts. When in difficult times, I don't necessarily see a way out, I just know it will come … at some point. I have desired to escape from life for a while, although not by doing something that risks death. My own concept of "escapism" on occasion has come to me while driving. I think about getting into an accident that would hurt me just enough to be hospitalized and taken out of reality for a little while, where I don't have to worry about anything—mainly because I would not be able to do anything. I also welcome the attention and care I would receive, and because it would be related to something physical, it would be okay. During my difficult times I definitely don't want to die. Taking a long vacation would probably do the trick, but when not feeling well even the idea of planning a trip is far too overwhelming.

As far as I can understand, contemplation and ideation about wanting to end one's life is generated by multiple factors, including total despondency, disappointment, hopelessness, despair, and one's own belief that their own shortcomings prevent any change in their situation. The feeling that this difficult time is temporary and will pass does not exist. Life becomes far too painful to even imagine any type of future that will not involve extreme anguish or a hellish existence. A plan to attempt suicide is seen as the only option when it appears there is no way out, no way for change to occur; continuing on in the midst of this misery does not seem possible.

To assume that suicide is merely a selfish act is only to admit ignorance as well as a lack of empathy and sympathy. Unfortunately, suicide as an act of selfishness is a very common view. When I was at the University of Pittsburgh studying sociology, specifically in the class Youth and Society, I wrote a research paper that focused on something I could not wrap my mind around: adolescent suicide. The year was 1988, and I really wanted to understand how life could look so bleak that one would want to take his life. Admittedly I, too, thought there must be a selfish component to suicide, as that was what I had heard so often when the subject was broached; it made sense to me logically. At this point in my life (four years postdiagnosis), I had not really considered the correlation of the incidence of suicide with bipolar disorder; I just wanted to understand people better and how and why life was so difficult for teens when they had what seemed to be their whole life in front of them.

However, as I have continued my thought process on this topic, an idea has occurred to me that contradicted what I thought all those years ago. I wonder if for teens, the concept of having their whole lives in front of them could actually play a role in their ultimate suicide ideation: thinking that they have their whole life ahead of them may actually mean that this notion of despair will continue *forever,* creating a feeling of hopelessness, and perhaps that feeling could lead to the actual event of suicide.

What I learned two decades ago has not seemed to change all that much. Although we may be better at pinpointing who is more likely to attempt and commit suicide, as well as ways to prevent it, the numbers of attempts and successful suicides are still shockingly high.

Two major causes of death and morbidity worldwide are suicide and suicide attempts. A statistic from the American Foundation for Suicide Prevention documents that suicide is the tenth leading cause of death in the United States, and in 2009 there were 36,909 reported suicide deaths. Strikingly, suicide was noted as the fourth leading cause of death in adults between the ages of eighteen and sixty-five, and more specifically, studies also show that a staggering 25–50 percent of patients with bipolar disorder make at least one suicide attempt.[2]

According to the Centers for Disease Control (CDC):

A combination of individual, relational, community, and so-cietal factors contribute to the risk of suicide. Risk factors are those characteristics associated with suicide—they may or may not be the direct causes. Risk factors [include]: fam-ily history of suicide; family history of child maltreatment; previous suicide attempt(s); history of mental disorders, par-ticularly clinical depression; history of alcohol and substance abuse; feelings of hopelessness; impulsive or aggressive ten-dencies; cultural and religious beliefs (e.g., belief that suicide is a noble resolution of a personal dilemma); local epidemics of suicide; isolation, a feeling of being cut off from other people; barriers to accessing mental health treatment; loss (relational, social, work, or financial); physical illness; easy to access lethal methods; unwillingness to seek help because of the stigma attached to mental health and substance abuse disorders or suicidal thoughts.[3]

The CDC also reports that "protective factors buffer individuals from suicidal thoughts and behavior. [These measures include] effective clinical care for mental, physical, and substance abuse disorders; easy access to a variety of clinical interventions and support for help seeking; family and community support (connectedness); support from ongoing medical and mental healthcare relationships; skills in problem solving, conflict resolution, and nonviolent ways of handling disputes; cultural and religious beliefs that discourage suicide and support instinct for self-preservation."[4] Also, as far as medication treatments are concerned, lithium is the only drug that has been shown to reduce the risk of suicide and suicide attempts.[5]

Mental health professionals are educated to have a comprehensive knowledge of mood disorders, but unfortunately such providers are not always easily accessed. For example, it is often months before a patient can get a first appointment with a mental healthcare professional. Primary care physicians are also trained in recognizing the signs of mood disorders and suicidal thoughts, and when it is appropriate, they can refer the patient out to a mental health professional. Unfortunately, even when all the best measures are available, it does not guarantee a positive outcome.

Addressing the impact that bipolar disorder can ultimately have on one's life in relation to suicidal tendencies is something I felt was necessary to include. Due to my lack of personal experience, I desired to seek out someone who would be willing to share his or her personal account of how this illness impacted the person to the point of attempting to take his or her own life. While at an annual mental health conference in 2006, I met a woman named Lisa. When Lisa and I began to share some ongoing and past issues with bipolar disorder, I also shared with her that I was writing a book about my experience with the illness to help to provide hope to others associated with the illness. While sharing parts of her story, Lisa then opened up to me about her suicide attempt several years prior. I asked Lisa how she felt about sharing this experience with others. She willingly agreed, because she too had the desire to create understanding and to help others who find themselves in similar situations.

Lisa's Story

I am currently forty-eight years old. I was diagnosed with bipolar II when I was thirty-five years of age, after experiencing seven severe depressions and two hypomanic episodes. In addition to bipolar II, I was also diagnosed with attention deficit disorder (ADD) and obsessive compulsive disorder (OCD). I do not recall being depressed in my childhood or adolescence. Any recollection of my initial situational depressive state began with the divorce from my first husband. The onset was situational but did not pass with time.

I married for the second time in 1990 and quickly became pregnant. When I was six months pregnant, I was diagnosed with a condition that caused me to go into preterm labor. After three days of labor, I finally delivered my baby girl three months premature. Tragically, after twenty-three hours fighting to keep her alive, my precious baby girl passed away. That was when I experienced my first deep clinical depression (although it was not diagnosed as such at the time).

My obstetrician recommended I see a psychiatrist and gave me a referral, and after just one visit, I was given the diagnosis of postpartum depression. No medications were prescribed, and the psychiatrist did not recommend I continue any treatment—so I didn't. I thought I could take care of things on my own. I was not dealing with the depression at its core and ultimately was only fooling myself in thinking I was over it. I tried to go on with my life, such as it looked. In hindsight, I was most likely in denial, as even with my prior depressed states, I did not recognize them as being severe enough to seek treatment.

I had two more daughters, the first in 1992 and the second in 1994. Before I had my second daughter, I was taking care of my mother-in-law, who had numerous health issues. She passed away days after I gave birth. This death was a huge loss to me because of our very close relationship.

At the time, my second husband was an active alcoholic who could not keep up with the bills for our family; he was verbally and emotionally abusive, and emotionally unavailable for support. I continued to go into semidepressed states and managed to get through them.

By 1996, with terrible finances, two children, no mother-in-law, and my husband actively drinking, I had lost fifteen pounds. The chaos of my emotional, unstable state had me feeling overwhelmed and completely anxiety-stricken. I was not sleeping or eating and was smoking cigarettes and drinking coffee. I was consumed with worry and fear.

I decided to look up another psychiatrist, and when I went to see her, I was diagnosed with bipolar II, ADD, and OCD. She started me on an anxiety and an antidepressant medication. By this point in time I had experienced seven clinical depressions and two hypomanic phases. I now had support from my psychiatrist, medication, and a work friend whose mom was bipolar II. This friend was important because she chose to understand rather than judge. I did not have family support at the time.

As I began to learn more about my various illnesses, I realized the environment I was in was not healthy for me. I moved south, to be close to my parents and two sisters. I left my husband and took my two young girls with me. I wanted to start a new life, and with the physical proximity of family, I believed this would be a good option. And it was for a while.

Meanwhile, up north my husband was utilizing the court system to threaten to make us move back. The custody battle went back and forth for a year and a half. In January 1999 I was forced to pick up everything I worked for down south and go back north in order not to lose full custody or lose the kids altogether. I did not have family, a therapist, or a support system there. Further, my husband was harassing me, threatening to keep the girls longer than his allotted time if I did not do something to his liking. This was an abusive and controlling environment, which was why I originally moved away.

I filed for divorce when I first returned up north and found an apartment to live with my two girls, separate from my husband. I collected unemployment while working intermittently as a waitress and drawing and testing blood per diem. My unemployment ran out quickly, and I had no health insurance for my medications. My soon-to-be ex wanted me to move back in with him and restore our marriage, and I just could not stomach that thought. Thankfully, the divorce was finalized that same year.

During this time, while in the start of a hypomanic state, I met a guy that I worked with in the restaurant who was on crack. I didn't even know what crack was, but because of the state I was in, I decided to try it one time while in his company. In my normal state of mind, I would not have experimented with it. This one-time event seemed to trigger the hypomanic episode even further, and after coming down from this elated state, the onset of depression reappeared.

For two weeks during this depression, I had suicidal thoughts for the first time. I was no longer on psychotropic medication, my financial status was below poverty level, and I had no family support in the immediate area. I felt like the walls were caving in on me. I was not sleeping, and my thoughts were racing for a good two weeks. I was telling myself, "I just want to go to sleep. If only I could just sleep!" I just wanted the consuming worry, fear, racing thoughts, and depression to stop. I was thinking about what I could do that wouldn't be so painful to make it all stop.

I did not consciously want to kill myself, but I knew I needed some way out. Irrational thinking accompanied my mixed depressive and manic states. I saw my provider, but I did not tell her (or anyone else) about my thoughts of wanting and needing to escape, and I gave her no reason to question me about harming myself. I had no funds to continue treatment or medication. At our last meeting, the doctor wrote a prescription for my anxiety. I filled the prescription only because my ex-husband paid for it.

Soon after filling the prescription, I asked my ex-husband to take the girls for a few hours so I could clean the apartment and have some peace. My ex-husband knew I was very agitated, and he respected my wishes and took the girls. I then took action: I drank a glass of wine and swallowed seventy pills: fifty antianxiety, fifteen of an antidepressant, and five of an antipsychotic medication. (That was all I had left.) I had followed through on my plan for sleep, knowing it could most likely kill me. The only way to accomplish the temporary solution of sleeping was to pursue the potentially permanent solution of death by overdose. I was hoping I would not die (this is why I left my apartment door unlocked, in hopes that someone would find me), but as irrational as it sounds, I wanted the opportunity to rest or sleep with no interruptions or responsibilities for a good two months and then get up and return to living again.

It was my ex-husband who found me and called the ambulance. I woke up days later in the intensive care unit of the hospital. They put me on a mood stabilizer, an antianxiety medication, and an antidepressant. My mom came up north to see me in the hospital. I stayed there for a week, and she then signed me out and took me back home with her. The girls stayed with my ex-husband; they remained with him for one year.

My mom's support for me was about protecting me: she thought if she could control my behavior and support stabilized living, she could control the illness that was consuming my life at that point. She did not understand depression, even though it was in her family. Still, in the midst of her lack of understanding, she was there for me. My father, on the other hand, told me to forget about the past and the depression and get over it. (Interestingly, my fraternal twin was diagnosed with bipolar disorder five years after me, so it was definitely in the family.)

After my suicide attempt, the best way I can describe my emotional state is being in a cocoon. The medications blurred my thoughts and actions. I couldn't drive, I cried every day, and I could not even fill out the necessary forms for social security disability insurance (SSDI). I was stuck in a place I could not get out of or move forward from.

My mom requested I begin to look for a job. Although it had been just three months since my attempt, she thought I was all better and was actually putting her own timeline for recovery on my health. (At this time my parents were also covering my medical and insurance costs.) I tried to get back to work. I worked as a phlebotomist in a private lab close to my mom's house. I was soon considered eligible by SSDI and was able to collect some disability insurance money, and I had Medicare for my health insurance.

My mental illness interfered with maintaining a job; I have either quit or been fired by many. My emotional outbursts would often be the cause of the trouble. I would go off on someone and would not stop, not realizing I was doing it.

Eventually I regained custody of my girls and then later remarried in 2002. Life has finally been peaceful. My current husband is wonderful and gave me the moral support I needed to go back to college to obtain a higher degree. He also has given me the support that has helped me to eliminate thoughts of suicide today. This support is also a result of having the correct medication, living a healthy lifestyle, educating myself in regard to the illness, and being actively involved in a support group. With all this support, my faith, and positive outlook, I do feel that my suicidal thoughts may never come back again.

As Lisa explains, she wanted out, and her way of getting out was to put herself to sleep for as long as possible, even risking death. For Lisa, this was her way to cope, and as a result of this illness, it was her best and possibly *only* way of responding to her perception that she would never get better. "The line between suicidal thoughts and action is not as clear as it might seem. A potentially deadly impulse may be interrupted before it is ever acted upon, or an attempt with mild intent and danger of death may be carried out in full expectation of discovery and survival. Often, people want both to live and to die; ambivalence saturates the suicidal act. Some wish to escape, but only for a while."[6]

Lisa's situation embodies so many facets shared by those who contemplate suicide, and that encompasses many people who have bipolar disorder: death of someone close (specifically family members), difficult or abusive married life, custody battles, financial difficulties, an inability to share with her therapist the deep level of despondency and the idea of suicide as an escape, feelings of inadequacy to alter or change the situation she found herself in (perhaps stemming from knowing she could no longer afford treatment, so not seeing the point of sharing), and the pain of imagining a future in a constant state of extreme anguish. Combined with a genetic component for bipolar disorder, these many factors could have been cyclical triggers that fed into her many depressions and some hypomanic episodes that could have ended tragically in her death. For many, death *is* the end result.

When in recovery from a physical illness, there seems to be a great deal of value for life. The same priority could easily be placed on mental illnesses. Proper and accessible treatment is essential, and by providing it, the number of suicides has a chance of decreasing. When I wrote that paper back in 1988, one of the goals set by the Public Health Service was to lower the rate of suicide among youth by 1990. Unfortunately, approximately two decades later there has not been much change. If we value the lives of human beings and start with the young, we can hopefully save lives, both the young and old alike.

Chapter 10
Believing What You Hear: Labels and Beliefs

A LABEL IS SOMETHING that is conferred upon a person or a group for identification in order to set one apart; a belief is a subsequent thought or idea associated with the label. Reciprocity exists between these two terms, and too often a label takes on the meaning of its associated beliefs. When opinions become truth and correlated assumptions become fact, the results can be damaging.

Most of us have created and adopted all sorts of labels and beliefs at some point or another. A label need not be negative, but once given it usually sticks.

I am most concerned with the commonly accepted labels and beliefs attached to people with mental illness. When it comes to mental illness, particularly in regard to bipolar disorder, I think the tendency has been to accept the labels and believe much of what is told to us without taking into consideration their truth or validity. Too often fear and a general lack of understanding play a role in shaping the awareness of what bipolar disorder is and what it looks like.

If a person is labeled mentally ill, that person is set apart and becomes different from those without mental illness. The diagnosis of mental illness in and of itself is a simple medical truth; however, a person diagnosed with mental illness is subject to disapproving societal opinion. The mental illness label is usually negative and carries significant disparaging connotations. Such an opinion-oriented label has nothing to do with the diagnosis itself or the person diagnosed.

The assumptions associated with mental illness are what often initiate the reaction by many to hold that person at arm's length: he is crazy; his judgment is skewed; he is not to be trusted; he is incompetent, unreliable, lazy, reckless, and damaged. Such assumptions become entrenched as factual character traits.

Societal indulgence given to such opinions and assumptions renders the person diagnosed with mental illness with a serious set of new concerns (notwithstanding the medical attention and personal commitment required to treat the illness). When a person is constantly referred to as mentally ill, all the negativity surrounding the labels and beliefs becomes internalized.

A bias is then set up for a diagnosed person to feel separate or different in the sense of not being normal. When people walk around not feeling normal in their own skin, they often feel they are not deserving of all the things any other person is. They may begin to doubt themselves, question their competence, or feel shame for being "less than." Confidence dissipates and self-esteem declines. What they believed to be true about their self is under scrutiny by outside influences as well as internal misgivings.

Not feeling worthy is a common feeling to those living with mental illness, and it may affect every aspect of life, from relationships to feeling confident enough to obtain and maintain a decent job. There are so many people with mental illness who have so much potential, but they do not reach for or succeed in their goals because they feel held back and pushed down (both from outside themselves and from within). Judgment received for what the person has no control over leaves its mark.

More often than not, the intensity of the internalization of the label is at its highest when a person with bipolar disorder is at his lowest or most vulnerable: during a depression or when coming down from a mania. (This can also occur when the person is experiencing a manic episode; although he may not seem to be comprehending, labels may still be internalized.) During this time of vulnerability, a person will most often question himself the hardest about his own character. Feelings of inadequacy, failure, or guilt arise due to the person's limitations (regardless of whether the limitations are biochemically induced and beyond his control). In a less vulnerable state, such thoughts may not carry the same weight, but they creep in and nudge at what he knows to be true about himself regardless.

It is no wonder to me why so many diagnosed with mental illnesses do not want to publicly disclose their mental illness when it comes with a label with such negative connotations. To become classified as mentally ill can be socially and personally devastating in its ramifications. Whatever there is to know and enjoy about that person is often set to the side or goes unnoticed.

The media does not seem to help the perception of bipolar disorder, often portraying it at its extremes and not showing the "well" person with bipolar. If someone who knows nothing about this illness sees the way it is portrayed on television, of course he will have very negative and fearful feelings that further support the label it has been given. This is particularly so in stories reported on the news: in the quick twenty seconds of footage to report a crime, one hears that the criminal is also mentally ill. Newscasts do not go into further detail to explain why this aspect of information is relevant or that this is not the person's everyday behavior. Instead, the relevance is assumed that mental illness is equated with danger.

As the awareness of the very nature of mental illness continues to grow, one would hope its label and associated belief-laden labels may not weigh so heavily, but they are quite powerful. There is also a responsibility that comes upon those who have been labeled to prove the very nature of the labels incorrect. Defending oneself in this regard can be a lifelong process and perhaps one that never fully gets completed, depending on the deeply rooted impact.

I have listened to, taken in, accepted, countered, and confronted the compounding mix of labels and beliefs that not only hindered my own personal growth but also reinforced the stigma that still exists about this illness. The negativity or labeling of a person as bipolar without regard for his personality and character traits has been something with which I continue to have a problem. This is not just specific to me but is true for many struggling with this illness.

My experience has shown me that many labels result from a lack of understanding. Just because a person does not have an understanding of a mental illness does not make negative labels or beliefs any less hurtful or less of a struggle to overcome. Because this illness is genetic, bipolar disorder is not a choice. Gaining an ability to control the illness, rather than the illness controlling you, requires tremendous effort to understand the workings of the illness, medications (and their continual adjustment), awareness of triggers, and what supports and inhibits balanced and productive living. There is no quick fix. Overcoming the diagnosis, coping with the frustrations of trial and error, and maintaining the ability to keep moving forward with a myriad of frustrations relative to the illness (never mind the routine ups and downs of life) is no small feat. Commitment to health becomes an essential factor of daily living.

When I was first diagnosed with bipolar disorder at seventeen, my life split into two categories: prediagnosis and postdiagnosis. Prediagnosis was a time of unquestioned normalcy, a natural progression with my peers, and daily expectations and disappointments. Postdiagnosis was a time of new fears surfacing that I would be viewed differently, and revolved around regaining and maintaining a sense of normalcy.

Up until my first hospitalization, I was naïve to any specific notions or ideas about mental illness. The only thing I knew about mental illness came from books, movies, and hearing about someone's distant relative who was locked up in a mental hospital because he or she was crazy. For me, the word "crazy" created a normal versus abnormal separation, and abnormal meant institutionalization (even for life) to remove that person from society. I was not concerned that this extreme applied to me—I was discharged and I got better—so I really did not know what to expect when I returned to school after leaving the safety of the hospital. I did not even know what bipolar disorder was prior to my own diagnosis, and it appeared to me that no one else at my school did either, so I did not know what comments would potentially be made about the witnessing of my manic behavior and the fact that I was away for a month afterward.

When I initially returned to school, I already felt different because I had this major event that happened to me and not to others. To me it kind of felt like me versus them, and I felt set apart. While trying to make sense of who knew what and trying to get back to where I had left off, I still had concentration issues and tremors as a result of the medication I was taking. I was very self-conscious and concerned that my classmates might notice. My friends (and even the students I did not know well) seemed to be very accepting of me, and things went back to normal as they had been before I got sick. To me, this response was pleasantly unexpected due to the very nature of high school students.

According to my brother (we attended the same school, and he was two years younger than me), the majority of students did not know what happened for two reasons: one, we had over twelve hundred students in the school, so many people would not have seen me (or known me for that matter); and two, I was only acting differently for a few days, so if anyone did witness any odd behavior, it would have been my close friends and those who were in my classes (and it was not every moment that I was acting differently). The awareness of what was going on with me was somewhat limited, although to me, after returning, it may as well have been the whole school who had witnessed me prior to going to the hospital. That was my perception, anyway.

As much as I appreciated the rapid acceptance and not feeling judged, I looked forward to the opportunity to have a fresh start at Michigan State University that fall and continue toward my goal of maintaining normalcy. Uprooting and moving to a new place puts a person with this particular type of illness in a position that lends to their anonymity, and they can choose when, with whom, and where they want to share their illness. Now I would once again be in line with my friends, doing what they were doing, and not be behind with classes. Unfortunately, that feeling of normalcy lasted only about a year before I was once again manic, behind, and different.

These cycles of coming in and out of feeling normal due to the mania occurred four times in six years. Following each manic episode, I had to rebuild my self-confidence and make up for lost time, only to have the mania creep up on me again. Each manic episode was a reminder that I had an illness because it would interrupt the normalcy I had created (and recreated) for myself. At the time, I did not see the manic episodes as the stripping away of my self-esteem; instead I simply faced each episode as an isolated incident and dealt with it as needed to move forward again. I saw it as a function of the illness. It is only in hindsight that I see the deeper, long-lasting effects to my self-esteem by the continual need to rebuild over and over my relationship with myself, others, and the illness, as well as the practical aspects of continually feeling the need to be in line with my peers.

The longer lasting effects on my self-esteem show up in a variety of responses I have experienced in regard to this illness, including defensiveness, guilt, shame, and controlling behavior. I have come to realize they are all natural responses to my diagnosis. It was important to me, however, to find a way to move beyond these feelings and reactions because I thought they were holding me back from experiencing the full possibilities of healthy living within the context of my diagnosis.

Early on I was very defensive about my mania, particularly whenever I was accused (that's how I saw it) of being sick or manic; at that time the mania was the only side of the illness that had presented itself. I felt as if I was being attacked for doing something wrong. I was unable to separate my actions resulting in negative consequences as a result of the illness, from the illness itself. Even just admitting the illness was back was my fault, too. When being questioned as to whether I was okay in regard to the illness, it did not feel as if anyone was truly concerned about me, just punishing and accusing.

I was most sensitive to my father's comments. My perception was that when my father suspected I might be going into a manic high, he would ask in a certain, somewhat suspicious tone, "Lizabeth, are you okay?"

I would respond, somewhat sarcastically, "I don't know, Dad, are you okay?"

Every time he asked, I would cringe and get this awful feeling that I was not being trusted or that I was being judged. I was trying so hard to keep my normalcy intact and therefore would get defensive, not just because I was trying so hard in my commitment level with medication adherence and awareness, but also because I did not want a manic episode to happen, and I did not want my father to be right that something was indeed wrong.

In actuality, these feelings of judgment and condemnation were more likely to have been my own internalized beliefs and certainly not what those who cared about me were thinking. I know that the questions from my dad arose out of his love and care for my well-being, but that was something I was not able to see or understand at the time. I now realize that this defensive feeling has carried throughout my life since age seventeen; the root cause of my defensiveness is connected to my response to the bipolar disorder.

I now see that how this question is asked, as well as in what context it is asked, makes a difference to me. This question has always been perceived by me as if my dad was actually saying, "I don't think you are okay." These questions would also arise if I was displaying genuine enthusiasm, or even if I was simply in a hypomanic phase. I wanted them to allow the situation to play itself out and not be all-consuming with every little detail of my behavior. It was so important to simply live my life without feeling like I was constantly under a microscope.

Once I was able to articulate my sensitivity to my dad regarding the repetitiveness of this question, he seemed to understand and discontinued asking that question in that tone. Perhaps that also might be due to the fact he had not sensed those warning signs that he inferred to precede a mania. This has made a difference because it removes one more stressor in my life, and it also seems to reinforce that I am fine. I think my parents knowing that I am fine has always been very important to me, as has been their approval. Perhaps that stems from me not feeling like I was doing my best in their eyes because of the illness and all the problems I caused when I was sick. So much seems to lead back to the illness.

Now I feel it is me who asks the questions to myself, not someone else. It's my inner voice that seems to be in check whenever a warning sign may arise. Most times I am just being hypervigilant, but periodically I need to call my doctor or adjust my sleep. I have not experienced a manic episode since 1990, so those four manic episodes in a six-year time period had a very long-lasting effect on me.

In addition to the defensiveness, for much of my life (but on and off) I have felt guilty for what I put my parents through as a result of my bipolar disorder. I often felt that I took years off their lives. My parents probably did age with what they had to deal with during these manic phases. It was not until recent years that I was able to come to terms with my guilt. An enlightening conversation for me occurred with my mom while the two of us were on our trip to Sweden together, a little over eight years ago. I told my mom how guilty I felt for both her and my father being put through so many trials in dealing with my illness all those years ago. My mom's immediate response was that she was my mother, and there was nothing for me to feel guilty about because of my illness. For her, a mother loved her children unconditionally, and in my case, she never saw me as a burden. I realized I had internalized my guilt; I had never experienced my mom expressing any type of frustration, annoyance, or a complaining comment like, "Not this again." She never felt anything but love for me. My mom's straightforward honesty helped to remove the weight of guilt I had been carrying for so many years.

Both my parents have since shared that they were never embarrassed by my actions; rather, they were scared, concerned, and saddened that I had an illness that would require not only hospitalization but also strict attention to medications and lifestyle modifications. For my parents, love and support were first and foremost.

For as long as I can remember, even before the onset of the illness, I have always been very hard on myself and have set very high expectations for myself. Being hard on myself has never been my best attribute, because I am first to find fault with what I do or leave undone. This can also be difficult because, as a result of my illness, where I want to be in life is not always possible and can therefore lead to feeling like a failure or that I'm just not good enough. Feelings like I'm not where I should be arise more predominantly with the depression, but I have also had these same feelings as a result of the manic episodes. With the mania, the feelings of failure to stay on track and needing to catch up and regroup occurred once the mania was under control; with the depressions, these feelings occur both during and after the episodic cycles.

While in the thick of my depressions, there was time to think and worry about how I would get out of this and how I would ever get back to my old self. After the anxiety of how to cope with everything, and as I began to get better, guilt would begin to settle in the form of doubt about my own intentions by taking an easy way out (needing sick days here and there) and not being true to my job at 100 percent. Doubting the truth of who I was continued to remain a component of the depression.

Contributing to my own feelings of doubt, I also experienced a questionable motive put forth by a psychiatrist when I was a student at the University of Pittsburgh. The situation occurred during the fall term. I did not feel well and felt that I could not cope. (This happened periodically with the seasonal change to shorter daylight hours; I now recognize these symptoms were the effects of SAD. As a result I would sometimes drop a class or take an incomplete.) I was again in a position to consider dropping a course.

This particular psychiatrist suggested that my pattern of lessening my workload meant that perhaps I feared success. Could this be yet another belief that gets attached to this illness? At the time I thought this to be such an odd question—of course I wanted to succeed! I wanted to succeed at being productive throughout the term and to finish my courses. That was my goal. But I did think about what the psychiatrist said, and I questioned some of my subsequent psychiatrists whether this fear of success applied to me or not. They did not think there was any merit to it, and neither do I—now.

I think what may have led to this line of reasoning is that when you are going through the warning signs and symptoms leading to an episode, be it mania or depression, things get so unbelievably difficult that alleviating the stress is really the only way you can see to get out, and often that may lead to quitting certain things that are too overwhelming. I think this is a commonality for many of us who have this illness. I know people without the illness may also go through periods of time when they are overwhelmed and want to give up; however, what differentiates this for someone with bipolar is the magnitude and longevity of the overwhelming feelings. What often results in these circumstances is that a learned response kicks in and creates doubt about whether it will be possible to move through it or whether it will put you into a spin. It is difficult to differentiate between what will pass and what will lead to a full-blown manic or depressive episode.

I now realize that there are other alternatives to giving up or quitting projects in order to alleviate the stress. The key examples for me are an in-depth phone conversation with my psychiatrist, with the possibility of making some changes including adjusting sleep patterns, exercise, medication, and maybe even taking a few days for a time-out to remove myself from the situation and gain a chance to see these options take effect before deciding on the next step. In addition, it has also been helpful for me to talk to certain family members and friends; doing so provides the encouragement or support to not let my own self-doubt or guilt dictate my actions.

Shame came into play within my first years of diagnosis. Shame is a painfully distressing emotion that ran deep and severely clouded my sense of worth. Shame was fueled by my complete and total embarrassment of lack of control, particularly with the mania that I had to face over and over. My sense of shame also contributed to my defensiveness. My manic episodes really had a snowball effect, each episode reinforcing that I had this unpredictable illness and was damaged. Knowing that both my high school and college peers had seen me in this manic state of mind gave me some sort of complex—I don't really know how it couldn't.

In later years, experiencing the depression was easier for me to accept. This did not mean I was more accepting of my illness per se, but I was more accepting of the depressive component. The depression creates less embarrassment for me, mainly because I see depression more widely accepted today; it is discussed more candidly than the extreme highs and lows of bipolar. Also, depression has been discussed more openly over the past twenty-five years since I was diagnosed, therefore making it not as difficult for me to share with others. It is my thought that many people experience depression, know what it is, and think they have some sort of understanding of it. On the other hand, regarding the extreme highs and lows of bipolar disorder, awareness is on the rise, but this awareness has not begun to catch up with the lessening of bipolar stigma.

Overcoming this shame of mine has been a battle. Feeling shame for who I am is a rough concept to wrap my head around. On a conscious level it does not make sense to me that I was ashamed for something I was not able to control. Today, however, my sense of shame has lifted due to a greater acceptance of myself. Outgrowing the fullness of shame has taken a very long time for me, but overcoming its stronghold has come with being more comfortable with who I am, believing in my own value, and ignoring the negative labels and beliefs that come with mental illness.

For the most part, I am now okay with talking to others about my illness, and this is mainly because I have been able to manage the illness and lead a productive, healthy, and happy life. However, even today, there is a small part of me that sometimes worries about others' acceptance and perception of me. Although my fears have lessened, there are those times—for example, at a new doctor's office when telling them what my medications are and my diagnosis—I sometimes wonder just what goes through their mind at that moment. I don't want to be thought of as a bipolar person. I want be thought of as me.

More often I experience a level of comfort after revealing the illness to someone and hearing the response that they are very surprised. My first thought is a positive one: it's a nice compliment because they see me as a regular, everyday person. My next thought is not so positive: the response confirms to me that many people's perceptions or experiences with a person with bipolar disorder are not of a person who is leading a somewhat normal and productive life. Unfortunately, it is more common than not for others to picture a person with bipolar disorder as someone who is not in control.

Another area of response to my illness was the sense of wanting to be in control of my life. This was due directly to the fact that I was not in control when manic. Even though the true manic periods of my life probably add up to a couple months, the aftereffects totaled up to much more time—years, actually. If I really think of it, it has been in the shadows of my life ever since. One specific example of how this has shown up for me is that for many years after my first manic episode, I had a tendency to do whatever I could to not exhibit any behaviors that others could interpret as manic. Therefore, I was overly careful with my money and my excitability. I wanted to appear to be okay at all times. Although much of this may have been a subconscious response, I actually thought I needed to be in control and would constantly keep my behaviors and responses in check.

I purposely overcompensated by going in the opposite direction of what mania looked like. My controlling behavior to this extent inhibited my true spontaneous nature; by controlling how I acted, I felt like I could minimize others' perceptions of my illness (and mental illness overall).

Today I do not do this as much, but to a certain degree it still exists deep down. For example, I find that even though I have the money to spend on certain things, I still sometimes stop myself and think, "Uh oh, is everything okay?" even though I am sure I am not manic or beginning to go into a mania. Checking in with myself is a conditioned response based on my one-time overspending experience during my second manic episode in 1986, twenty-five years ago. I seem to not allow myself to be completely myself, or what my definition of normal should look like. There are many people who do not have bipolar disorder and go on spending sprees, and it is not seen as a problem or a red flag.

At this point in my life, I am much more comfortable with who I am, and I don't analyze my behavior as much in terms of how it relates to the illness. For the most part, I feel that I have overcome the defensiveness, the guilt, and the shame. I think the controlling aspect will always be a part of me, largely due to my need to be responsible and accountable for my health and overall well-being. I sometimes have to remind myself that with or without this illness, I would never have been perfect.

Sharing about my bipolar disorder on my terms was not always the case when I was dealing with this illness as an adolescent and early adult: people saw me in my manic states that could not be hidden, and then I would need to return to that environment. It is important for people to know me first before I tell them about my illness, and this is my choice to make. Having the choice to tell whom I want and when is a powerful and important option for me. The reason I want people to know me for me is because I am me, not my illness. I want people to see me as Lizabeth, not as a person who is bipolar. Over time, this idea of waiting to tell people has lessened as my comfort level with myself and this illness deepens. I still feel that when I tell someone about my illness, it is a privilege for them because I am sharing one of the most personal things about me, something that is very near and dear to my heart.

Up until I was seventeen, I was not labeled as manic-depressive— or mentally ill or crazy, for that matter—and no one has ever said there was any indication of any odd behavior prior to my first manic episode. Although there was so much more for me to learn in my life and growth was inevitable, at this point in time I was still a person whose personality was pretty much formed. If anything, the illness took away some of my personality for fear of the labels people have when they hear a person has bipolar.

Living with the label of having bipolar disorder for over twenty-five years, accepting that I have a mental illness, and having this mark for such a long time has had one accumulating, all-encompassing effect: feeling damaged for pretty much my entire adult life. Breaking down the barriers that cause the negative feelings generated from such biased labels is very difficult; but now, after so many years of working at it, I do believe that the sense of feeling damaged because of my bipolar disorder has gone away. I am different, yes; I have an illness. But it does not make me damaged. Accepting myself for who I am has finally freed me from the idea that I am less than others.

Chapter 11
Questioning Your Value:
Internalizing Societal Stigma

A BIPOLAR DIAGNOSIS LEADS to increased risk of internalizing societal stigma toward mental illness. Prior to diagnosis the individual may or may not have held the stigma to be true. The individual may or may not have really thought about it unless it affected someone he knew. Once diagnosed, however, the individual becomes vulnerable to believing it to be true about him. Far too often this leads to the desire to hide the illness and creates a barrier to seeking support. Without support, feelings of shame and inferiority compared with the rest of "normal" society begin to strengthen and take hold.

I believe the desire not to reveal one's illness to others is a normal response. On the one hand, it is a private and personal piece of information to share. On the other hand, if the stigma can be kept at bay, it's one less thing to deal with.

What many do not realize is that a bipolar disorder diagnosis also comes with the requirement of time and energy to stay committed to adherence to medications, psychiatric appointments, therapy, and numerous lifestyle modifications. Taking all of this in at once is exhausting. The added desire to explain and express what bipolar disorder is and feels like in order to create understanding is often too much to take on.

We may be able to dodge the intention of the external critic, but our internal critic does not let up; the severity of the stigma of mental illness is too pervasive. Reconciling for ourselves what is true becomes essential. This is extraordinarily difficult when we doubt our own abilities, feel our self-esteem erode following manic and depressive episodes, and feel guilt and shame for not being able to do enough, well enough, or fast enough to return to our goals.

Living with a secret you feel is shameful—whether it is rational or irrational—is an excess piece of baggage that gets heavier and heavier to keep hauling around. To hear others laugh or comment negatively about something that relates to your own situation and circumstances only fuels the desire to keep the secret. It saddens me that the stigma of mental illness causes the one who has it to feel like they are not worthy of others' time, attention, company, or friendship, and they actually live in fear to keep this dark secret within.

After twenty-five years of living with bipolar disorder, what is clear to me is that by releasing the hold of stigma within myself for myself is what ultimately preserved my own sense of well-being. For me, taking all this on one step at a time over these years enabled me to pursue treatment, express openly what this illness is for me, and keep a sense of balance rather than continually beating myself up over something I did not bring upon myself. My response is what I have control over, and I take on this responsibility.

In the beginning, I saw my diagnosis of bipolar disorder as an illness that needed to be managed. But as the episodes of mania continued, it was solidified that I had this kind of craziness that had become a part of my life. With each episode the layers were compounding: I had an illness that was in charge (reinforced each time the uncontrollable odd behavior would rise); I was feeling pushed backward even while taking my medications and doing what I was told; and I had to continually catch up and rebuild my sense of self and self-esteem. These aftereffects also included how I felt about what I had put others through, once I was told what had happened and what they witnessed. Whether or not they were bad things did not matter—it was my perception that mattered.

Later on in my depressions, there were feelings of worthlessness and a sense of failure at copping out and letting down those I worked with because of my need to take time off. This was the other end of the pendulum, behaviorally and emotionally.

Overall, when combining these feelings and emotions, the core issue was that I had a mental illness—and at the end of the day, that was something I did not want to be associated with. I knew logically I was a good person with good qualities, but the trump card was that I had a mental illness with no guarantees.

For as long as I have had the diagnosis of bipolar disorder, there have been numerous occasions when I have heard others comparing illnesses of the mind to physical illnesses. No matter what anyone will try to tell you, they differ tremendously. About twenty years ago a family friend (also a psychologist) who helped me through some difficult times tried to compare my illness to diabetes or a broken leg. I really felt it was not a fair comparison. Trying to compare a person's mental illness to a person's physical illness runs the risk of insulting the person with mental illness, no matter how many similarities you may find. You can look at a person with a broken leg and see the physical problem, and it seems fair to say that a broken leg is "acceptable" and one does not get looked at as odd because one has a cast. In fact, compassion is often given to the person when others witness them hobbling along. I also recognize the seriousness of diabetes, but it does not carry the same type of negative associations as mental illness because it's something physical, not an illness of the brain.

When I first heard this comment comparing my mental illness to a physical illness, I had only experienced the manic part of the bipolar disorder, and the actions that resulted were not recognized as normal. The manic person's behaviors are often described as crazy, out of one's mind, taking part in reckless behavior, spending excessive amounts of money, and talking incessantly and rapidly, making it difficult to follow a conversation. So yes, I can understand how this behavior from the outside can seem crazy; however, many people lack the understanding that the unnatural behavior is a part of the illness, and with proper care and committed diligence, can be managed. Further, a person diagnosed with bipolar disorder does not need to be branded as crazy as they pursue a productive, healthy lifestyle.

Those who love and care about a person dealing with mental illness are faced with difficult and frustrating responsibilities, too:

they suffer and contend with worries, concerns, fluctuating moods, and negative reactions to medications, all while trying to create safety, desiring to control the illness, and more. The response of others to physical illness and mental illness in general is similar in that there is the desire for the affected person to feel better as well as a sense of helplessness when one is not able to do anything.

Sometimes those who have not experienced the extremes of bipolar disorder are quick to dismiss the severity or impact it has on the diagnosed person. There is pressure put on those who are ill to hurry up and get better, manage it quickly, and move on. I feel it is imperative that those who are diagnosed do not take on the notion to dismiss it as well, or not take it seriously even if those around them dismiss or minimize it. As hard as it may be when those close to us lack compassion or understanding, our focus on health and well-being needs to remain strong. Those diagnosed with bipolar disorder should be aware of the difficulty that lies within another's understanding of the illness: it is simply an inability from a lack of personal experience of what it is like to be tormented with something that is at times so difficult to control. It is the hope of us with bipolar disorder that others will be open to trying to understand what occurs as a result of this illness.

Although both empathy and compassion help considerably with bipolar disorder, it is not something one can understand fully unless one experiences it personally. Although the family members and friends who experience the results of a loved one's mania or depression on a day-to-day basis can try to identify with what they see and grasp the concept, understanding what is going on in a person's mind as they are experiencing the illness is entirely different.

A person with depression may appear to be withdrawn and quiet, but it is possible one's behavior is not as outwardly obvious as the behavior one exhibits while in a manic episode (this would be to the average stranger, not by someone you know well). When referring to depression specifically, this reminds me again of how important it is for anyone suffering from it to be aware that others who have not experienced it will have a difficult time truly understanding the illness and how we who experience it actually feel. A common misconception about clinical depression is that many think it is just about being sad. Many people who have not experienced clinical depression feel they can relate because they too have been sad and depressed about situational things that have gone on in their own lives. The assumption would be that clinical depression is this same type of situational depression, but at a deeper level.

At its onset, clinical depression is not about being sad; it is the chemical imbalance in the brain that causes the depressive symptoms (which include sadness). My experience is that when I begin to spiral down, the chemical imbalance has been put into motion. It may have been triggered, but that is not always necessary. When people experience depression, others often see them as being selfish, only thinking of themselves (a "poor me" mentality). Actually, that is okay initially, because it is very difficult to see beyond oneself. To others, it may seem that you should be able to get over it or pull yourself up by your bootstraps—perhaps this is what *they* do to handle their own situational depression. The amount of energy it takes to try to explain the nature of clinical depression to a person who has not experienced it is so difficult when in a depressive state, it often can't even be expressed. Often this leads a person to feel the need to be alone.

I realize there is so much more information available about bipolar disorder and depression today, and with so many people more aware of it, it does make a difference. However, although the stigma attached to mental illness may have diminished in the minds of some, it is still running rampant in the minds of many. There is a greater depth of understanding in the field I work in as a professional in pharmaceutical sales and the nature of the physicians I have called on (many being psychiatrists). This also holds true with many of my friends who are either also in the medical field or have gained some sort of deeper understanding through me sharing the details of my illness. These people I have interacted with, however, do not represent the general population or those who experience mental illness. The pharmaceutical company I work for manufactures both antidepressants and bipolar medications. The company tries to work at the acceptance of these illnesses as well. I, in turn, see that attempts are being made to slowly chip away the stigma, but my company, the pharmaceutical industry as a whole, and I do not represent the opinions of the world.

There is an enormous amount of responsibility placed on the person diagnosed with bipolar disorder. As mentioned previously, bipolar diagnosis is not something a person has control over; what can be controlled is the response. And not everyone responds the same way or finds the effective levels of medication necessary to regulate the illness. It requires a constant awareness of medication level adjustment and lifestyle changes. Also, some people are medication resistant, and others use more natural ways to treat their illness. The hope is that each person diagnosed responds in the best way he knows how with the tools at his disposal. There is no guarantee regarding treatment, only a personal commitment to health.

The first example of stigma that was experienced by my family and me occurred almost two years after I was diagnosed, while I was in the midst of a manic episode at Michigan State University. It was many years after this experience that my mother shared her own recognition of the stigma I was experiencing in the outside world. My mom told me she received a phone call from my roommate's mother, calling to complain about the overall stress my manic episode caused her daughter. She spoke with bitterness, saying how dare my mother allow me to emotionally abuse her daughter. My mom knew that even with my adherence to my treatment plan and awareness, my manic behavior carried with it unfortunate incidents, and clearly I did not mean to harm anyone else. My mom tried to explain the nature of the situation and the illness, but to no avail. To my recollection, my roommate did not say anything to me to convey any concern she may have had regarding my behavior; if I had hurt her I would have wanted to have known. We were not good friends, only a little more than acquaintances. It was clear that neither my roommate nor her mother had understood, or really even tried to understand my bipolar disorder, and that any upsetting behavior (being high-spirited, talking fast and incessantly, jumping from subject to subject, struggling with confusion, running from one thing to the next, and even hosting the champagne party) was not intended to be abusive or inconsiderate to anyone. I would also think it was clear that there was something wrong with me and that I needed help. I wish they could have seen it that way.

This phone call was very upsetting to my mom. I could still see how angry my mom was after all this time about this woman who had absolutely no compassion for me, just resentment toward *us* for affecting her daughter. Hearing about this incident all these years later was extremely disturbing to me, too. My first reaction to this conversation was anger, and then it shifted to sadness in two different ways: first for my mother and the way this affected her and to see the response of anger still the same from so many years ago; second for anyone with the illness who deals with the outside world's lack of understanding (and their lack of desire to learn more), seeing the pain it causes those with the illness.

I have continued to witness an overall lack of sensitivity toward mental illness. One evening back in the early 2000s, I was at a party and one of my friends started talking about a cousin who had bipolar disorder. She continually pointed out how crazy he was, and she actually made fun of him as she told stories about his outlandish behavior. At first it took everything in me to not say anything; none of these people knew about my own experiences with bipolar disorder. Further, I did not even know some of those present. We were in the kitchen, and there were about eight of us standing around the table. I soon realized, however, that I couldn't listen to it anymore and not respond. I finally asked her if he takes his medication, and she said no. I told her and the others that when people with this illness are compliant with their medication, their illness can be very well controlled and they can live a very normal life. She knew I worked for a pharmaceutical company promoting an antidepressant and that I was well-informed about depression-related illnesses. I was also very confident in her not even considering that I knew something about it because of personal experience. I started to think about how their perception of bipolar disorder was that the person was crazy, and those poking fun were certainly not sensitive enough to even consider that someone in their presence (or one of their friends or family members) could have bipolar disorder. I guess this can also be considered as a form of ignorance (as well as a lack of sensitivity and empathy).

I acknowledge that although I did not reveal any personal experience in order to save face, I did take a step forward and say something in her cousin's defense, pointing out that it was not a laughing matter. To some, this situation would seem an opportune time for me to step up and share my bipolar disorder. It is, however, only more recently that I would even consider doing this. This lends to my own acknowledgment of the stigma that exists, which I am trying to whittle away. The idea of having others judge or look at me differently was not something I was ready to address head-on a decade ago.

This brings me to the most personal example of stigma I have ever experienced directly, which occurred only a few years ago. I typically do not tell people I meet that I have bipolar disorder, at least until I feel they know me for me. Not that long ago, one evening at a banquet I met a man named Jim, whom I ended up talking to for a couple hours. We soon discovered we had many mutual friends and had been at the same places on multiple occasions; it was a wonder we had never met before. On the evening we met, I ended up sharing with him that I was very busy writing a book in my free time, in the midst of working a full-time job. Naturally he asked what the book was about, and I joked with him saying that if he's lucky, some day I would tell him. I'm not sure why, but I did end up telling him about the book that night. He was not all that familiar with bipolar disorder, but he certainly did not seem scared of it at all. That night he got my phone number, and he did call me; we soon went out on a couple dates, got along well, and connected very quickly.

Soon after we started dating, I received a phone call from Jim while I was in San Diego at a conference. He had just spent some time with some of our mutual friends. During the phone conversation he said those dreaded words: "I have to tell you something." It did not sound good, but I could not imagine what it could be. I hardly knew him, and we had only been on a couple dates. Jim then told me that he had mentioned to one of his friends that we had been out on some dates, and soon others in the group found out too. Two friends pulled Jim aside and informed him that I was a great girl ... as long as I stayed on my meds. Wow! They'd never seen me off my meds, and they'd never seen me sick. I had not been manic since 1990, and that was years before I'd met them. They had never seen me depressed either.

Jim could have run for the hills, but he didn't. He wanted to give me a chance, and after he shared it with me, he seemed to let it go. I, on the other hand, did not. When he realized how upset this made me, he really felt bad for sharing it, but I was so glad he did. I was angry and hurt and really could not believe it. I could not believe that in all my years of dealing with this illness, and my fears of what people thought all those years ago, something like this would come up when I was in my early forties. I was mortified. This was a very personal attack on my character.

It actually took me a couple years to let it go, in part because of how shocking it was, and also because I still saw these individuals several times each year. It was on the forefront of my mind when I came into contact with them, and I did not want to interact with them at all. Finally I decided to forgive and let it go—it was not worth giving more attention to something so negative. I never discussed this with either one of them, but I could not help but wonder what their motivation was for telling him something like that.

Things could have turned out so differently with Jim, had he been scared away by their gossip … but we are still dating. It shows a lot about his character that he gave me a chance regardless.

Do people mean to be cruel, or do they simply not understand? I'm not really sure in this case, but it was a very good example of what people with these illnesses have to deal with. How odd that I chose to tell Jim about the illness before our first date. If not, who knows what he would have thought. Thank goodness something like this had not happened before. I am very blessed not to have heard people talk badly about me prior to this. Hearing something like this at an early age (or earlier in my diagnosis) could have been very damaging. It greatly affected me even after I had become comfortable with who I was.

I am fortunate that those in my life, especially my family, have been patient and taken the time and effort to be very supportive of both my manias and depressions, even though they do not always understand them. They have not shown any stigma toward me, and that helped tremendously just knowing that it did not exist in my inside world (i.e., family). The response of my family, close friends, and support groups has allowed me to express my stigma-related feelings in an environment of safety. I no longer feel shame or inferior to others simply because of the bipolar disorder. Discussing my concerns of guilt for what I feel I have put others through (particularly my family) resulted in love and concern—no one was resentful, and it was me who needed to address the guilt. My actions were part of the illness. The support and encouragement of others, as well as my own maturity with this illness, is what led me to recover my own sense of value.

Today I accept myself for who I am with bipolar disorder. I rather like myself with the illness. I have grown because of the illness. I am a more compassionate, empathetic person when confronted with the suffering of others, whether it be an illness, poverty, or just getting the short end of the stick. For some reason I have become a huge fighter for the underdog and the disadvantaged. Perhaps this stems from feeling the same way and working to turn that around to help others.

The last step for me regarding stigma exists with those who do not know me well or those with whom I work. If they discover I have bipolar disorder, what will they think? That simple question opens me right up to that fear of stigma—the external critic, not the internal one. It is up to me to recognize the stamp of disapproval I may receive and to accept that they may be unwilling to try to understand and to see me as a person. If this is the case, then it's okay for me not to worry about their opinions. Stigma is meant to hold another down, to judge one as inferior. If I allow myself to view myself within the negative confines of stigma, I am the one who loses out in the end. With all the new breakthroughs in medicine, I thought there might be a breakthrough with stigma as well. For the most part, I have been wrong about that.

Chapter 12
Fearing Rejection: Dating Relationships

I HAVE HAD MANY short-term relationships, ranging from one to six months, interspersed with several long-term, more committed relationships. Whether or not the duration of the relationship was long, it was often intense; intensity and passion are part of who I am. I would not go beyond a first date if I did not feel a connection from the beginning. As I have come to learn, the intensity that I possess in most things is not uncommon to those with bipolar disorder; in fact, it seems that it is one of the personality traits that are shared among us. Knowing this helps to better understand how I interact and respond in relationships and why I tend to give them my all.

My dating experiences and relationships have definitely been affected by my bipolar disorder. Because I was diagnosed at seventeen (still an impressionable age and before any real serious dating began for me), much of my adult life was spent feeling damaged, in the sense that because I had bipolar disorder and therefore a mental illness, I was not good enough to be with someone else.

Not recognizing my full sense of self-worth in regard to dating relationships is difficult and comes with sad acceptance, especially after years of successfully managing this illness. This is where the term "emotional scarring" resonates for me, with layer upon layer of negative, shaming emotions carrying through and building upon one another over the years. Logically I knew feeling damaged was not the truth of who I was, but beneath all the positives I had achieved lay the cloudy feelings of self-doubt and a lack of self-worth.

I can now objectively look back and realize that internally there were two belief systems in opposition with one another. The first was that if a man really loved me, he would unconditionally accept me as I was with bipolar disorder. The second belief undermined the first belief: the label this illness produced in me was that I was not whole and complete; I was unworthy and incapable of being loved the way I wanted and needed, because I had a mental illness.

Until several years ago, I was not entirely aware of my competing subconscious belief systems, and why for the most part I was choosing men who were emotionally unavailable. I believe this was because I, too, was not ready for a relationship that included vulnerability and emotional intimacy. I sought out men who were reflections of how I felt about myself. Being attracted to an emotionally unavailable man—and the limitations that this type of relationship brings—eliminated for me the risk of being rejected because of my illness. Ending dating relationships in the early stages enabled me to avoid this risk as well. Although I wanted an enduring relationship on a conscious level, my subconscious belief had the final say and dictated many of my decisions, thereby creating relationships that were potentially doomed from the very beginning.

The cycle of my relationships, particularly in the beginning, would often run the same way. If a man did not know I had bipolar disorder, then the relationship would continue. However, with the intensity of feelings I would experience, I would find myself pulling away or sabotaging the relationship before I had the chance of being rejected for something over which I had no control. I was creating much internal strife about what I wanted versus a lesser type of relationship I thought I had to accept. In order to decrease the possibility of rejection solely due to the illness, my relationship algorithm was that once we had both said, "I love you," then I would tell him about my bipolar disorder.

There are so many levels contained within the stigma of mental illness and being rejected regarding relationships. On the one hand I accepted the illness for myself (even with the sense of value limitations); however, in order to let someone else in, they too needed to understand the illness and all that it entailed. The problem I was creating was that I did not even give the men a chance to make the decision for themselves—I made the decision for them instead by placing on them my own preconceived notions of how I would potentially be judged and dismissed. My choice to withhold information about my bipolar disorder stemmed entirely from fear. I did not want anyone to see me as an image of mental illness in a negative sense. I wanted them to see me for who I was and not just see the illness. In essence, I was contributing to the stigma even though I was not aware of doing so. I had taken what I had learned and experienced regarding stigma, and I transformed its meaning for myself in a way that spilled over into my relationships with men.

I experienced several very serious and long-term relationships beginning in my late twenties, where we had both said, "I love you." Within these serious relationships it is hard to determine whether the bipolar itself played a role for the men. My inclination is not to believe so, because I know it was accepted and I was not made to feel differently than someone who did not have an illness like mine. It was not until these later, long-term relationships that I was finally able to break down the barrier I had held on to deep down for so long: that my illness would be the ultimate reason for a breakup. I learned that sometimes two people just are not meant to be together.

These relationships also revealed a side to me that represented commitment, staying power, and stubbornness (and even a bit of naïveté to think that people will eventually change). I believe in love and have not wanted to give up a relationship that has so much good in it. I also see that in continuing to hold out, I compromised what I deserved—that same commitment in return. Without full commitment, I had only part of a relationship, and that was certainly not enough. I was willing to hold out for hope. I suppose that even though many things are worth fighting for, there are limits. No matter how much a man loves me, how wonderful he says I am, or how great he treats me, without full commitment it really isn't enough. Certainly full acceptance of the bipolar disorder isn't enough for me to stay.

It has taken me a long time to believe that I am worthy of being in a committed relationship and deserve to be an equal recipient of love. Dating an emotionally unavailable person is something many experience on the learning curve of how healthy relationships work. What I was doing was condoning the unavailability due to my own doubts of worth for a fully invested relationship. I let some relationships run past their time because of this. My hope is that those reading this can recognize their own self-worth and live it out fully. For me, I am happy to have realized this at all, even though it has taken much of my adult life.

Having been diagnosed at such an early age afforded me perhaps the best advantage that would impact the ability to sustain and maintain all types of relationships: the ability to learn, understand, utilize, and put into practice the tools to manage bipolar disorder to lead a productive, healthy, and happy life. However, having to live with the bipolar label, and consequently having a mental illness, has meant over twenty years of feeling the brunt of these labels, having spent the majority of my adult life feeling damaged, and not feeling worthy of being loved by a man. Had I not been diagnosed so early (or at all), I may have felt better about myself (for not taking on the stigma for so many years). To be clear, I realize the advantage to early diagnosis outweighs the severity of dealing with so many unknowns about mood stability and judging myself without a specific reason (e.g., not feeling normal and not knowing why). Overall, I certainly feel more fortunate to have been diagnosed early on.

I also find it very interesting that a good 20 percent of the men I have dated or have been interested in had a past girlfriend, wife, or family member with bipolar disorder. (That number could actually be higher.) I am unclear if these men were drawn to me, or I to them, because they felt comfortable or something felt familiar in me, as I had never spoken about my illness with them. I shared my curiosity about this information with one of my psychiatrist customers, and she agreed with me that this pattern had to do with the familiarity—but even more so, they were drawn to my positive energy. That was such a great compliment, especially with all I have been through and how I viewed myself in the past (which was more negative).

In regard to marriage and children specifically, many women with bipolar disorder (including myself) have expressed at one time or another that they do not want to have children for fear of passing along the bipolar gene to their child. A psychiatrist from Johns Hopkins School of Medicine, Glenn J. Treisman, MD, PhD, shared something I will never forget and wish I had heard many years ago. Dr. Treisman said that wiping out the bipolar gene would be like removing color out of our world. He also said that people who have bipolar disorder add so much to our world and society with their creative and intellectual gifts.[1] Knowing that so many famous, intelligent, and creative people have this illness definitely helps me to see that I am in good company, but apparently I know that has not been enough. Dr. Treisman was emphatic about pointing out that not having children due to the possibility of passing on the bipolar gene would be more of a discredit rather than a credit to society.

If much earlier in my life I had heard someone (especially a professional) talk so positively and with such conviction about those who have the illness and how life would be so dull and less fruitful without them, I think I really would have seen the extraordinary traits that come along with the illness. It would have made me feel more valued and more worthy of a healthy male relationship, and perhaps I'd even believe that a person who would be involved with me would be very fortunate to have me, not just because of the person I am but because of my illness, too. Today I do feel that way to a degree, but not in a conceited way, more of a confident one. Having such encouragement at such a young age would have made a difference, and I feel Dr. Treisman's words are an amazing way to sum up this illness. Hearing them even twenty years after diagnosis, they still made a difference and made me feel better about myself. It is my hope that this will resonate with others.

Chapter 13
Sources of Strength: Supportive and Healthy Relationships

FOR ME, PEOPLE AND relationships are what life is really all about. Supportive and healthy relationships are those that are developed and then maintained and sustained over time; they are relationships built on trust and with people on whom you can depend. These relationships are not a one-way street—there is mutual give and take. In general, healthy and supportive relationships make life a bit smoother. When speaking specifically in regard to my bipolar disorder, not being judged by those who care helps significantly with acceptance of my illness, because the stigma is minimized. It is extremely helpful to know that people care and are ready to help with whatever it is I need, even if it is just to listen.

As with other mental illnesses, people with bipolar disorder often have trouble maintaining healthy and supportive relationships. Often the outrageous manic behavior is the cause, but damage can also be done during the deep despair of depression, and sometimes between the two extremes. Many with bipolar disorder lose friendships, spouses, and family members. Even jobs are lost, not only due to behavior or lack of performance on the job, but also due to how one reacts with other coworkers or supervisors. At the heart of it all, the responsibility of a person with bipolar disorder lies within himself. Even when actions are done when we are not in our "right minds," if we do not take the responsibility to stay well, then the illness alone is not to blame. Certainly there are times when a person is not capable of getting the help he needs—or even knowing he has an illness of extremes. In these scenarios, the illness would be to blame. It may be even more difficult to repair and restore relationships when harm has been done because the person is not clear why he acted or responded the way he did.

Supportive and healthy relationships have been a predominant part of my life. These relationships are with family and friends (from long ago and more recent) as well as from work, church, support groups, and mental health-related conferences. I feel that my desire to have relationships and the benefit of early diagnosis both played major roles in maintaining those relationships. Many of these relationships were formed and sustained before the illness presented itself, others were during and between my manic and depressive episodes, and still others continued following relatively controlled maintenance of the illness. Many of my friends are not directly connected to my bipolar disorder, although I certainly have made many additional friends as a result of the illness. This illness has not robbed me of my ability to sustain relationships.

My family and friends love me and support me outside the illness. They do not perceive me solely as a person with bipolar disorder, but rather as a person with a personality and characteristics they desire to know and share time with. Perceiving me for all that I am—while also understanding and being compassionate for the responsibilities of bipolar disorder—is an essential component in long-standing, meaningful relationships. This feeling of not being judged, which I have been fortunate enough to experience, helps to maintain my sense of balance with this illness, so that my focus is on getting on with living while contending with the illness. My family has always been a very strong, positive support system and also provides me with the unconditional love I seek to experience. With the onset of bipolar, this was a crucial foundation. My siblings continue to be a big part of my life; they have all supported me in their own ways, but each expresses compassion and love.

The relationship I have with my mom is more of a traditional mother-daughter relationship, where she has always been a role model for me. She has demonstrated love, compassion, honesty, and trust—

all characteristics I admire in her and, in turn, instilled in myself. She is a pillar of dependability and integrity. My mom is a selfless person, and she always put her children first. She is the epitome of motherhood, and I am privileged to have her as my mother. I was fortunate to be able to share something extraordinary with her that took place during my adult life.

One of the best trips (if not *the* best) I have taken was with my mom. We took a trip to her birthplace, Köping, Sweden, and were gone for about twelve days. The quality time we spent together visiting relatives and my mom's friends showed me how much she was loved and appreciated. We spent hours reminiscing about her childhood and family memories, and we laughed a lot. I felt I got a true glimpse into her past, and I truly loved learning and taking in all I could.

The relationship I have with my father is also one that I cherish. My dad and I are alike in many ways, including our sense of structure (although it seems to come more naturally for him), our humor, our sensitivity, and our love for interacting with other people. My dad has also been my financial go-to person all my life, and he has given me much sound advice to help me get to where I am today financially. One of the best things he has taught me (and this is by example) is that every person should be treated fairly and equally; no one is better than anyone else. My dad is so friendly and says hello to everyone. It sounds so simple, but I don't see this general lack of prejudice in many people.

I feel a special bond with my parents—a bond that has been there since childhood and that continually grows. They have always loved me throughout the good and the bad. Supporting me through my illness, in addition to all the ways it has affected them, is more than I could have ever hoped for from two parents. They have never complained to me about how difficult and draining it was at times for them to deal with my illness. I have always loved them, but feeling this sort of unconditional love from them has shown me how this kind of love has no boundaries.

As an adult I was privileged to get to know and spend quality time with my father's parents. My mother's parents did not live as long, and unfortunately I did not have the opportunity to know them in the same way. After spending time with my dad's parents for many consecutive years after high school, I developed a close and strong relationship with my grandmother. We shared lots of things about our lives with each other, and she even shared some things no one else knew. There was a mutual sense of trust, and it really did become more of a friendship.

My relationship with my grandfather took an interesting turn upon the death of my grandmother. He lived another eight years, and during that time we developed a great respect for one another; the friendship that my grandmother and I shared seemed to transfer over to him. I continued to visit him at their home in Florida, and after he fell while riding his bicycle at eighty-nine, I decided to visit him more frequently than just once a year. That same year, after more falls, he moved into an assisted living facility followed by a nursing home when he was ninety-one.

While Grandpa Schuch was in the nursing home, I learned more about him than I had over the many years I had already spent with him. I was privileged to have the opportunity to spend the entire month of October 2004 with him prior to him passing at age ninety-three. I was in Florida during my typical difficult fall time, and the trip was therapeutic in many ways. Grandpa and I spent many hours just talking or sitting together. He was a great listener and really took it all in. His wit was very charming, and his mind was still quite sharp.

My bipolar disorder did not impact or change the love, care, and respect he had for me. Whether he understood it, I'm not really sure, but it was something we did not really discuss. He just accepted me for who I was and believed in me. He always told me how proud he was of me and that I had a good head on my shoulders and knew what to do and when to do it. It's amazing that this person who was such a huge part of my life was not fazed by my illness, and neither did his opinion of me change because of it. I know how much he appreciated me, and he told me that often.

In the final years of his life, my grandfather affirmed a valuable life lesson for me. He had overcome many obstacles beginning with his childhood, yet he still remained positive and content, showing those around him that life was just fine no matter where you were or what your circumstances were. During those final two years he spent in a nursing home, I was able to witness the effect he had on those he interacted with by his example of how to treat others with kindness and compassion, by listening and not judging—no matter what. He was a true example of a loving, giving, and wonderful human being.

Supportive relationships have also come through people who are a part of my life as a direct result of having this illness. These are people I have met from the support groups and various mental health conferences I have attended over the years. I have made lifelong friends this way. These are people who understand, and therefore they lend a very unique type of support. The connection we share is often instant and very different from any other. These relationships are very valuable to me

Throughout my life, other friends have played a very important role that has directly affected the quality of my day-to-day living. They have been there for the good and the bad times. These relationships have been maintained without the illness being the central aspect of our shared experiences. Having their support and their acceptance of me really helped me in living with bipolar disorder; they viewed me as a person first.

I still remain friends with one particular group of women from high school. There are seven of us, and we have known each other for over twenty-five years. They were all around during the onset of the illness, so they have seen me at my best and my worst. In the midst of all I went through, they always treated me with love and respect, and we all support one another regardless of any of our shortcomings. We had much fun in high school, and as we grew up and apart (in proximity), we remained friends, sharing in each other's good times and bad, including weddings, children, family tragedies, and the like. Although none of us live in the same city, and our lives are so busy that it precludes us from being in constant contact, we know we can count on one another if ever needed. Maintaining these friendships for such a long time is both unique and special; it shows how much we all value friendship.

After graduating high school and going our separate ways to college, one high school friend, Jean, and I both ended up back in Pittsburgh. We began to get to know each other better, and maintaining this relationship throughout our twenties—a time of transition, changing educational and career goals, and developing a greater sense of maturity—supported us getting into our thirties. Even more than a decade after I relocated to the DC area, we are still there for each other and maintain a strong friendship.

Together, Jean and I met five other friends in the Pittsburgh area. These five all met me after the illness and never experienced my extreme ups and downs. I told them about it, but it never really played any role in our relationships. They certainly were there for me if needed, but we all were there for each other for all types of things, as friends are. This group of friends was particularly special because we spent many years doing fun things together, including going to happy hours, spending evenings out, dancing and socializing, attending various Pittsburgh sporting events, having our annual summer Dewey Beach weekend, as well as other spontaneous getaways. Being a part of such a great group of friends allowed me to be my adventurous self, and no one ever considered my enthusiasm to be mania (because it was just enthusiasm). Those friendships have remained intact over the past twenty years. We are all still in contact and do still see one another, but as with my group of high school friends, proximity and busy lives make it harder to get together.

One other person (whom I also knew in high school) and I became close friends when I moved back to Pittsburgh. Diane and I shared much in common (including things related to depression), and we have been able to have an extra special understanding for one another that goes beyond our regular friendship. I continue to visit her when I'm in Pittsburgh. Having someone in my life who not only knows me from so long ago but also understands what I have been through has been a godsend. She does not judge me, and our relationship is built on love and respect.

In 1995, while at Dewey Beach just days prior to moving to the Washington, DC, area from Pittsburgh, I met several people who later ended up introducing me to a very large group of friends. Within that large group, a smaller group of friends emerged, and these are people I have spent much time with over the past ten years or so. These friendships have also been special in many ways. When I moved to DC, I knew only my brother and his wife and my friend Erin. I thought that meeting people in this new metropolitan area would be quite easy, but I soon found that was not the case. Meeting this group of friends as a result of going to a beach with my Pittsburgh friends was quite interesting; one group of friends led me to another.

Another valuable friendship actually grew as a result of me wanting to relocate from Pittsburgh to DC. Erin became my roommate and coworker at the same time. We have shared the good and bad, our hopes and dreams, our shortcomings and disappointments. Through it all, she has moved quite a bit, and at times we were not in constant contact, but the friendship has never wavered. She has been a true friend and someone I can be myself with at all times. She never judges and is always there for me when I need her. She accepts me for who I am.

My church family has also been an extension of my biological family. I have been an active member and have many friends there, both young and old alike. I feel very close to many of these people, who have become my friends and with whom I can share my faith. This type of fellowship helps to sustain my foundation of faith and is a vital part of my life. After telling some people from church about my illness, I received much love and support. Through sharing about my illness, I found others who have experienced some sort of depression—be it unipolar or bipolar, them or their family members—and it has been comforting to both them and me. They, too, have shown absolutely no judgment against me for having this illness, and they seem to have even more respect for me after knowing what I have been though.

Over the ten years I've spent working for the pharmaceutical company, I've developed so many more friendships. At first no one knew of my illness. As soon as I had to take time off work for depression, I did let some people know, but I never mentioned the bipolar part, just the depression. I had no shame about the depression, and I experienced no judgment from my coworkers, either. I more recently decided to tell a select few about my bipolar disorder. I did not want to be marked as bipolar in the workplace or take the chance, with them knowing, that I could potentially be jeopardizing my job in any way. As mentioned previously, a fear lies within me because

I have known other people with this illness (both in and outside my company) who have lost their jobs as a result of it. I did not want any more attention brought to me than already had been with my depression. A clear advantage to me not telling those I work with is that it has been great having people not know what I have been through. To those I have not told, I come across as normal. To the others I have told, I have found that I am still normal, too.

When I was first hired as a pharmaceutical representative, I met someone during the company training who I did not realize would become a lifelong friend. Her name is Sherri. When I traveled to North Carolina for training in June of 1999, Sherri was my roommate, and we had much in common. Having Sherri as my roommate made training so much more bearable, as it was very intense. We learned and studied for our training exams together, and in the midst of all the hard work, we had fun, too.

Our experience in North Carolina was just the beginning of a wonderful friendship between us. Now, over ten years later, even though she lives in Kansas, we talk on the phone often and see each other about once a year. Sherri is someone in my life who has been privy to just about everything. She is someone I have felt comfortable in confiding to throughout the years. We basically share it all with each other, no matter how bad we think it might be, and we seem to be able to give very honest and raw advice, or just listen when that is all that is needed.

Sherri is compassionate, kind, witty, and intelligent. She always seems to know what to say when I doubt my abilities and self-worth, and she reminds me of who I really am by reinforcing the good she sees in me. She's both giving and selfless without letting go of herself. She's a true friend. She has always been sensitive to my illness and has been willingly open to understand it; by doing so, she has helped me through difficult times with all the ramifications of my illness. Having Sherri in my life matters; by never being judgmental, she does not confuse me with the illness, thereby allowing me to be me, just as I am.

This brings me to the most important and most influential relationship in my life. I am referring to my faith and the relationship I have with God. Without this relationship, I am not capable of having any others. Through God's guidance and mercy, I have been able to find my way in this vast world. The relationship I have with God is similar to those I have with my family and friends, but with God there are no secrets: He already knows my heart and accepts and loves me as I am, faults and all. Having this friendship with God has not only brought me peace but comfort and joy as well. My relationship with God is a two-way street. Although I receive so much from God, I feel I strive to give back to Him in many ways too. I try my best to do as He has instructed us to do, and by upholding His Word the best I can, I feel I seek to give Him what He is asking of me. I have my shortcomings, but I continue to do my best in pursuit of who I think He wants me to be, specifically in the way that I treat others. I truly believe that treating others as I would want to be treated is most pleasing to God.

One of the interesting things I have only recently realized is that it actually has been me who has felt abnormal; this has not been expressed by those around me, and especially not by my family and friends. They have given me no reason to feel this way, and if anything, they have seen me in more of a positive way for how far I have come. This awareness, like a light bulb going off, further demonstrates all the years and layers upon layers of negative feelings I placed on myself as a result of this illness.

As I reflect back, I see how my family and friends have helped to shape my life. God has truly blessed me with people without whom my life would basically be nonexistent. I have gained much wisdom with age, and I know I would be at a different place without these supportive and healthy relationships in my life, and not for the better. I realize one of the more important things those close to me have shown is a genuine lack of judgment in connection with the illness, and this has been key. Notwithstanding the illness, but especially because of it, these close ties and relationships have offered deep and meaningful enrichment to my life.

Chapter 14
Family Connections: Genetic Predisposition

PREDISPOSITION FOR MANY ILLNESSES runs through a family's genetic makeup. A genetic predisposition for mental health issues can be traced through my own family on both sides, although the evidence and diagnoses are clearer on my father's side. Once I was diagnosed and subsequently hospitalized, I was made aware that Uncle George, my father's brother, also had been diagnosed with manic-depressive illness. Prior to my diagnosis I had not been aware of knowing anyone who was diagnosed with this or any other mental illness.

In past generations, psychiatric treatment was not as sought out and information was not as readily available as it is today. On both my father's and mother's sides, there were signs and symptoms expressed that were never diagnosed by a doctor or psychiatrist. I point to the issue regarding my maternal great-aunt in Sweden, who presumably died from drinking too much vinegar as a means of weight loss. This behavior may be attributed to an eating disorder or some sort of self-esteem issue, which may come into play with bipolar, depression, or anxiety, and it may therefore be a potential sign of mental illness. Also to this end, my paternal grandfather appeared to overindulge with his consumption of alcohol. To my knowledge, my grandfather never referred to himself as an alcoholic, although his behavior typified a functional alcoholic. Alcoholism was not prevalent in our family, and it was Uncle George who thought perhaps there was more to my grandfather's drinking habits.

In 1965, my Uncle George asked his father to accompany him to one of his psychiatric appointments. My grandfather was fifty-four years old at the time. Uncle George posed the question to the doctor of whether or not my grandfather had any discernible symptoms of mania or depression. The psychiatrist concluded that he felt my grandfather did indeed possess symptoms that would warrant the diagnosis of manic-depressive illness. My grandfather was not prescribed any medication or given treatment of any kind; however, the belief was that his excessive use of alcohol arose from attempting to self-medicate, to cope with his depression in addition to whatever stressors were currently going on in his life. (This was very common forty-five years ago and obviously still is today—in fact, 61 percent of those diagnosed with bipolar disorder have substance or alcohol abuse issues.)[1] My grandfather did not show signs of the extreme highs of mania, but perhaps he did experience occasional bouts of hypomania, which could have easily gone unrecognized. (I think they perhaps expressed themselves through irritability.)

Back then in the mid-1960s, the psychiatrist's response to my grandfather and uncle was that he theorized that manic-depressive illness was passed down from one generation to the next. This psychiatrist's personal view correlated with his own anecdotal experience that suggested genetic predisposition for mood disorders. At the time, there was little documented to support the doctor's personal belief.

Neither of my parents has been diagnosed with bipolar disorder, depression, or anxiety, nor do they have symptoms that have gone untreated. Two of my three siblings, however, have needed to manage issues related to mental health at some point in time. My brother, Douglas, has had no signs or symptoms whatsoever of depression, mania, or anxiety. My younger sister, Susanne, has dealt with anxiety that required medication years ago, and today exercise plays an important role in her wellness. My older sister, Debbie, still suffers with major depression.

Debbie experienced what she remembers as her first real bout with clinical depression in 1999. Several events of situational depression preceded this and most likely triggered the clinical depression.

Debbie first turned to the guidance of her general practitioner, as was the case for many when first seeking treatment. The doctor diagnosed her with premenstrual dysphoric disorder (PMDD) because productive living became more difficult for her and typically worsened just prior to her menstrual cycle. He prescribed Sarafem for her to take the week prior to her cycle. (Sarafem is a formulation of the antidepressant Prozac.) Symptoms of PMDD include "irritability, anger, tension, depressed mood, and mood lability (crying spells, verbal outbursts, or tantrums) to such a severity that quality of life is seriously compromised."[2] What distinguishes PMDD from other mood disorders is that the condition's onset and duration are related to the menstrual cycle.[3] Women with PMDD are also at a higher risk for developing long-term depressive disorders.

Within the next year, Debbie sought the counsel of a therapist, and shortly thereafter she began seeing a psychiatrist, who managed her medication for depression separate from the PMDD. In the subsequent years, she saw a number of psychiatrists, psychologists, and therapists, all who tried various medications and therapies, which have not yet successfully managed her diagnoses of PMDD, major depression, and general anxiety.

Thus, over the past ten years, Debbie's struggles with depression and anxiety have continued. At times she has been able to enjoy aspects of her life, but she seems to struggle in the midst of that enjoyment. Her battle with fatigue has made it difficult to accomplish many tasks, and her weight gain has been an issue that exacerbates the depression. She is also a perfectionist and therefore is very hard on herself. Not living up to her expectations for herself contributes to her sense of low self-esteem. She often feels overwhelmed, sometimes to the point of simply shutting down. Furthermore, she experiences irritability, anger, and even occasional rage.

For some time now, I have thought that Debbie has bipolar disorder type II. Given a strong family history of the illness, it is especially surprising that she was not seriously assessed for the disorder much earlier during the time she was under the care of a psychiatrist.

In fact because of discussions she and I had had regarding her symptoms and my own diagnosis, Debbie even suggested to her first psychiatrist, early in her treatment, the possibility of her having bipolar II. However this doctor, for reasons never clearly articulated to her, simply dismissed the notion as not plausible. Years later, in mid-2009, a new clinician revisited the possibility of bipolar II and gave Debbie that very diagnosis.

Not long thereafter, however, Debbie had a nagging uncertainty about this diagnosis and sought the advice of an expert in the field of bipolar disorder, specifically to try to assess if her bipolar diagnosis had been accurate. This physician carefully assessed her symptoms and came to the conclusion that she did not have bipolar disorder. He did note, however, that her symptoms do fall within the broad spectrum of the illness. For this reason, Lamictal continues to be part of her medication regimen and has quite effectively helped stabilize her rapid mood lability. (Although it is not indicated for depression, Lamictal is also prescribed for people who have difficult-to-treat depression—it is not solely prescribed for people who have depression related to bipolar disorder.)

Since this evaluation, in addition to major depression, anxiety, and PMDD, Debbie has received a diagnosis of obsessive compulsive disorder (OCD). Through the continued combination of therapy and medication, she and her doctor and therapist are working toward the goals of managing and even overcoming her illnesses.

On the extended side of my mother's family, it is still questionable whether anyone has suffered from some form of mental illness. At times signs and symptoms have been present, but it is not something that the family wants to discuss or acknowledge.

My uncle George (my father's brother) has two daughters, Allison and Tami. Although they have not been diagnosed with bipolar disorder, they each have experienced some forms of depression and anxiety. Throughout Allison's childhood, still now into her adulthood, she has had horrible stage fright and performance anxiety as well as a lot of OCD tendencies and other various concerns of perfectionism, body-dysmorphic issues, and insomnia. She experienced some depression on and off as well, but never so severe to the point of being nonfunctional or in a state of complete despair. For her, it is the anxiety that gets her into a bad place, and that anxiety (and the anxiety *about* the anxiety) can lead to depressive states. Allison has taken medication for her anxiety intermittently, and she is currently seeing a psychiatrist for medication management for panic attacks.

Tami struggled with mood disorders primarily during her adolescent years (sophomore and junior years of high school), during which time she was hospitalized and medicated for anxiety and depression. She was prescribed Xanax but found that she did not like the addiction she felt to this medication, so she opted for an alternative therapy in the form of biofeedback. (Her form of biofeedback was a form of learned response to stressors and anxiety: Tami's temperature and heart rate were monitored via computer so that she may mindfully control the relaxation response.) Tami found this alternative therapy to be very empowering and helpful. In fact, when she finds herself in stressful situations today (flying on an airplane, for example), she still feels that the skills she learned during those biofeedback sessions serve her well. Thankfully she has not had any recurrence with either the clinical depression or debilitating anxiety.

With my extended as well as direct family history set in place, this leads me to the family member whose life experience with this illness has been instrumental to my understanding firsthand the diagnosis and treatment methods that preceded my diagnosis by two decades. Understanding the way the illness has evolved over the years has helped me to gain insight into my illness and where I am now with it.

As previously mentioned, up until I was diagnosed with manic depression and began treatment for it, I had no idea that my Uncle George had this illness, too. We interacted with my extended family frequently when I was a child while living in Chicago, and then less frequently after moving away to Pittsburgh. Uncle George never gave reason for my siblings and me to think anything was ever wrong with him. We never heard anything about his illness or witnessed anything out of the ordinary.

After I was diagnosed with manic depression and learned that it was hereditary, it was not a shock that someone else in my family had it as well. I recall my Uncle George being very supportive from the beginning, but it was not until years after my own diagnosis that Uncle George and I discussed in-depth the similarities of our illnesses. Although we had a common diagnosis, our symptoms presented in opposing ways: Uncle George experienced hypomanic and major depressive episodes (now referred to as bipolar II); for my first sixteen years postdiagnosis, I only experienced full manic episodes, not the major debilitating depressions I experienced years later (now referred to as bipolar I). Uncle George and I understand a lot about each other's illness, and he continues to be a tremendous support for me, especially because he has lived with this for so many years and is very knowledgeable. He also has a very calming spirit and is extremely empathetic.

Because Uncle George was diagnosed in the 1960s, I was very intrigued to gain a clearer understanding of what he went through, his treatment, and how all this compared with when I was diagnosed in the 1980s. My uncle's first depressive episode with manic depression was in the fall of 1963, when he was twenty-two years old and had just started teaching high school. His trigger is still very vivid to him even though it occurred over forty years ago. He experienced a sudden cardiac-related abnormality called paroxysmal atrial tachycardia, whereby his heart rate sped up very rapidly. This was not a fatal condition, although it did require treatment with an IV of the drug adenosine, which was administered in the doctor's office. The condition reversed and has not been an issue since.

To him, though, the incident was so traumatic that he literally thought he was going to die, and he began to spiral down. He could not get death out of his mind, and from that point on, as he describes it, he was captured in a hellhole of darkness with no way out.

What Uncle George experienced was severe depression, and as it continued and worsened, he had to leave his teaching job for about two months. He was hospitalized for one and a half weeks, where he was misdiagnosed as catatonic schizophrenic. He was treated with a very strong medication that made him feel loopy, incoherent, and rather out of it. As soon as these side effects wore off, however, the full force of the depression returned. Nevertheless, his psychiatrist discharged him against the wishes of his family practitioner. Upon leaving the hospital he continued to take the medication prescribed by the attending psychiatrist. Uncle George's misdiagnosis may have arisen due to the similarities of symptoms between manic depression and catatonic schizophrenia. Catatonic schizophrenia is "a form of schizophrenia characterized by a tendency to remain in a fixed stuporous state for long periods [this would be the depression]; the catatonia may give way to short periods of extreme excitements [the hypomanias]."[4]

Uncle George sought out a new psychiatrist, and this doctor took him off those original medications and started him on a new regimen more suited to the treatment for the depression that gripped him. This new psychiatrist also correctly diagnosed him as manic-depressive, and Uncle George began to receive proper treatment and medication. Prior to being given medication, in an attempt to treat his severe depression he underwent three series (two treatments per series) of electroconvulsive therapy (ECT) over a period of two months. ECT is a treatment for a variety of mood disorders. The theoretical purpose of ECT is to activate a massive discharge of neurotransmitters in a rhythmical pattern to reset neuronal mechanisms in the brain to alleviate symptoms.[5] For Uncle George, this treatment was very effective. He was then prescribed Tofranil (a tricyclic antidepressant to treat clinical depression) and Butisol (also known as a barbiturate to treat anxiety and depression, among other things) for about ten years. Even with medication, he continued to experience hypomanias lasting for short durations, followed by deeper lows that lasted for longer periods of time. In 1974, eleven years after his first episode of depression, his doctor took him off Tofranil, put him on lithium, kept him on Butisol, and sent him on his way.

Uncle George was put on lithium without any medication supervision (which would be unheard of today), but his recollection is that he adjusted to the medication without any problems. In 1985 his doctor retired, and his new doctor kept him on lithium, took him off Butisol, and prescribed Prozac. Not long after this new combination of medications was introduced, the doctor took him off lithium because he was afraid that the combination of lithium and Prozac could contribute to a spiraling-up effect that could actually cause a manic episode. (Today evidence shows that some antidepressants have been known to precipitate a mania. It is not the lithium that would bring about the onset of a manic state.)

153

After seven years of Uncle George's Prozac-only regimen (1992), the same doctor put him back on lithium and took him off Prozac. The doctor now informed him that lithium did not contribute to a manic phase, and if anything, lithium reduced the incidence of highs and was a contributing agent in preventing lows. In 1997, Uncle George's doctor retired, and so he changed doctors once again. This new doctor took him off lithium for the second time but kept him on a very small dose of the Prozac. About two years later he took him off Prozac. Since 1999, Uncle George has been on no medication for mania or depression, and he has been free of any manic or depressive episodes since 1997. Overall he has had three incapacitating depressions, and for him, each and every episode of depression was preceded by an episode of hypomania.

In tracing back how genetics has played a role in the history of my bipolar disorder, not only has there been confirmation of it, but also the family link has been a very significant factor for me. Although throughout the generations there have been changes in diagnosis and treatment for bipolar disorder (including medication and therapy), many things have also stayed the same. To me, the biggest changes include increased awareness, better medications with fewer side effects, and better means for a more accurate diagnosis.

Although there have been struggles in dealing with the difficulties that accompany bipolar disorder, having others in my family with some form of mental illness (or components of it) has added to the support I have gained—and also to the support I have been able to give. My family also offers a true sense of compassion: they were and still are an instant support system and are readily available when I need them. Knowing I am not the only one in my family with this diagnosis has contributed to my recovery process.

Chapter 15
Maintaining Balance: Tips
on Productive Living

ACCURATE DIAGNOSIS OF BIPOLAR disorder is not always straightforward and clear. Bipolar disorder does not always present itself specifically (through a manic episode for example), and sometimes it can be misdiagnosed as clinical depression (unipolar) for years until a manic episode presents itself. One reason for this is that many people do not come in to see a doctor when they are manic because they feel so good and in their mind have no reason to seek treatment. It is more typical to seek treatment when a person presents with depression (whether or not they have experienced a manic episode).

Quite frequently a patient is treated by a primary care physician who is not specifically trained to treat bipolar disorder and does not typically have the extra time it takes to determine a proper diagnosis. Many times the patient is prescribed an antidepressant, and unfortunately if the patient has bipolar disorder, this may cause the person to cycle up into a manic episode. Often this is when bipolar diagnosis begins. Additionally, the symptoms of bipolar disorder can go into remission with or without treatment. However, without medication treatment, very often the symptoms come back—although when and for how long are always variables.

Therefore, when dealing with bipolar disorder, it is important to realize there are no definitive means of diagnosis that may categorize this illness with a beginning, middle, and end. With or without treatment, maintenance to promote the best possible outcome for wellness is never a guarantee. This is not to say one is doomed for life; rather, being in awareness of treatment options (medication and otherwise) to regulate wellness becomes an integral part of daily life. Bipolar disorder can be managed to the best of one's ability, although to achieve a productive, healthy, and fulfilling life, one must take the necessary personal steps to get there.

To the best of my understanding, in order to survive and thrive with bipolar disorder, I truly believe there are two golden rules that will enable someone with bipolar to begin to take the steps necessary to live a balanced and productive life. The first rule is to accept that you have this illness called bipolar; until you are able to do that, you will not be able to successfully seek treatment and incorporate other tools to keep you well. Once a person comes to terms with having the illness, then the next hurdle is to find the right treatment and stick with it. Therefore, the second rule is adherence. Lack of adherence to medications, therapy, and lifestyle modifications may lead to more frequent episodes as well as adding to the severity of the episodes.

I see in those struggling with this illness—and have been told this by mental health professionals as well—that both acceptance and adherence are probably the most difficult aspects for most people with bipolar disorder. Nonacceptance and nonadherence are also the main reasons people with bipolar disorder do not get well.

For me, both acceptance and adherence occurred relatively quickly. I know this is one of the reasons I have had fewer episodes than I potentially could have had. With the first psychiatrist's diagnosis that I was a textbook case manic-depressive, I immediately said, "Okay," and thus began my acceptance of this illness. With the knowledge of genetic predisposition also being a factor, a diagnosis like this was not out of the realm of possibility for me; I never doubted what my illness was. Thank goodness, because this meant I never stopped pursuing treatment.

Adherence was actually immediate. Perhaps this stemmed in part from my willingness to comply with doctors' wishes, something I'd learned at a very young age. When I was diagnosed at age seventeen, I was still impressionable, and doctors had always been authority figures for me. I also knew my behavior was very different, and I was able to distinguish between my normal behavior and how I'd acted the month prior.

I was very fortunate that both my acceptance of my diagnosis and my willingness to comply with recommended treatment occurred as soon as they did, although at the time I certainly did not realize how important these aspects would be to my future in living with bipolar disorder. Facing the many challenges that can result from experiencing the magnitude of manic episodes—which can last anywhere from days to months, with extreme mood changes switching from pure elation to anger and extreme irritability, and then dipping down to a very deep depression, only to then switch back to elation—would have been much more difficult for me without my two golden rules. Accepting the possibility for this type of roller coaster journey to be one's lot in life is a very difficult concept.

I have found the more I come to know myself, the more I have control over the management of my illness. When my treatment regimen is in control, I can get back to living again without living the illness all the time. After all, we know our own bodies and minds better than anyone, including our psychiatrists and therapists. Therefore, it is imperative to be open and honest with our medical providers so that they can give us the best treatment possible. Some aspects of our lives and behaviors are very difficult and even embarrassing to share, but it is important that these do not get in the way of total openness with the practitioners taking care of us. They need the whole story to successfully treat you, and this is only in the best interest of us, the patients.

When I speak of doctors as being authority figures, I also recognize that they are just as human as the rest of us and are capable of making mistakes. I have learned that no matter how much I respect their expertise, I still question things, and that is okay. I have also realized that I need to listen to what my body is telling me. I have looked back and seen that, unfortunately, I sometimes took a psychiatrist's opinion over my own gut feelings, not listening to what my instincts were telling me—and these incidences ended up in setbacks. I have since learned that I need to really trust myself and get a second opinion if things are not resonating between me and my doctor. We are all so different with different personalities, and it may mean working with several psychiatrists to find the best match for a doctor-patient relationship. It is always okay to change doctors. You cannot be worried about how particular you are being or how the doctor is going to react. It is important to do what you can to find a psychiatrist or therapist with whom you can be comfortable.

Understanding the role lithium plays in my treatment plan is very apparent to me now. My lithium levels have been below the therapeutic range for much of the time I have been on lithium. Even with such a low lithium level, it is evident that lithium is essential to my well-being. When I was first taken off lithium eleven months after starting it, I experienced a manic episode. Once back on lithium for sixteen years and then taken off it again, the almost immediate depression that followed proved that lithium also had antidepressive traits in addition to its antimanic properties. (The depression also may have been due in part to being taken off the lithium so abruptly.)

Nonadherence with medication is a common barrier that prevents balanced health for those with bipolar disorder. Lack of adherence may stem from multiple reasons and feelings. Some may be fearful of what the medications may do to our personality by stifling it in some way; others may fear the side effects of tremors, cognitive impairment, weight gain, tiredness, and having an "out of it" type of feeling, to name a few. Even once a person has made the decision to begin medication therapy, if the unappealing side effects do occur, he might stop his medication abruptly and be turned off by medication treatment for a long time (if not forever), rather than try another combination of medications. The person may not realize that all medications will not respond in the same way and that other adjunct therapies, like light therapy and supplements, are available and useful as well. Stigma may also play a role, because there is the fear of what others may think if they know a person is taking medicine and has a mental illness. Initiating any type of medication or treatment can be quite scary. Sometimes the prohibiting factor is financial: without insurance coverage for medications or psychiatric visits (or if one has a limited insurance plan), treatment may be out of reach. All of these reasons are valid.

Nonadherence can also stem from not wanting to lose the high feeling of the mania, and it can also occur due to not having the desire to be helped when deeply depressed. To this end, I would go as far as to say that it is often the illness itself that contributes to nonadherence, versus placing the full responsibility on the person. The conclusion that a person who has bipolar disorder must want to get better, and until he does he will not be able to be helped, is skewed. This is where the understanding of this illness gets extremely difficult for someone who has not experienced it. Once a person gets well and learns how to acknowledge and understand and cope with the illness, then it begins to become his responsibility; until then, it is not fair to place all the blame on the individual. We are not all born with the same coping skills or the same abilities to cultivate these coping skills. We don't all come from supportive families or have supportive friends, and not all of us have the financial means to get the help necessary for management of this illness.

Although there are many fears that may accompany the initiation of medication therapy, most often there are many more benefits. It does not mean that a pill is going to change things overnight, and it does not mean there will not be some undesirable side effects. For many, though, what it does mean is the beginning of newfound hope. With the help of medication, a person can be well on his way to healthy well-being, but medication alone is not enough.

In addition to psychiatric visits for medication and therapy, there are a whole host of behavioral modifications that I have discovered help me manage this illness more effectively. The safeguards I have put in place ensure a more stable and healthier lifestyle, thereby giving me the best chance of staving off some triggers that may contribute to either mania or depression. Disciplining myself in the areas of medication, structure and routine, sleep patterns, exercise, eating habits and nutritional supplements, light therapy, alcohol consumption, maintaining a good support system, spirituality, keeping well-informed with current treatments, and recognizing warning signs in regard to my illness are choices I have made to improve my quality of life.

Taking Medication Appropriately

Once one is willing and able to take medication, there is the added responsibility to take the medication appropriately, and this is essential to maintaining wellness. Unfortunately, doing so is not always the easiest thing to do. Even in midst of my strong adherence, I still struggle at times to take my medication correctly—there have been a few times when I take my morning medication at night and vice-versa. There also are some days that I cannot remember if I took it at all, and inevitably I take two doses in a row or miss a dose altogether. The result is that my entire day can be thrown off because I will have side effects that will accompany having too much medication too quickly or not having enough. My best solution is keeping a weekly pill container that has compartments for each day's medication. I do use it faithfully, but I still occasionally make a mistake. After all this time of taking my medicine, I still have to make a concerted effort to take it correctly. This just shows how easy it is to make mistakes with medication for bipolar disorder, even when you take it willingly.

Structure and Routine

For as long as I have had this illness, I have been told by my psychiatrists that having as much structure in my life as possible is good for my well-being. Having structure (e.g., having to be at a job at the same time every day, keeping consistent exercising habits, going to bed and getting up at the same time each day) helps to better ensure that I will keep a balanced life, be able to maintain my commitments, and keep stress levels lower. When there is an absence of structure, it is easier to get off balance, and this can further support the illness by increasing the amount of undue worry and stress. When I'm depressed it is very difficult to get out of bed in the morning and stay motivated; if I do not need to be in a specific place at a specific time, it is very easy just to stay in bed. Sticking to a schedule of some manner or fashion, such as with a job, can add stability. Also, keeping things in an organized manner (whether it be your living space, bills, finances, or a daily planner) will help to maintain order rather than chaos. What I have learned in my experience (as well as hearing it from many others with bipolar disorder) is that this is a common challenge for those who share this illness.

Sleep Patterns

Sleep can negatively or positively affect this illness. You can deprive yourself of sleep all the way into a manic episode, so getting a decent amount of sleep each night is very important; for many this means a full eight hours. (It is also important to note that mania can also cause sleep deprivation.) Getting too much sleep often can be one of the warning signs of depression, so it is important to monitor your sleep. Also, continuing with the theme of keeping on a schedule, going to sleep and waking up at the same time is very beneficial. The rhythm and regulation of adequate sleep helps maintain the body's natural wake and sleep cycles. From all I have learned about sleep from my current psychiatrist, I would venture to say that sleep is so important that without the proper regimen, it can hinder the treatment protocol prescribed. I truly believe that good sleep hygiene provides a strong foundation for managing this illness.

Benefits of Exercising

I know there are many benefits (both physically and emotionally) to exercising, and when I am doing so at least three to four times a week, specifically cardiovascular, I feel my best. Exercise is a natural antidepressant because of the release of endorphins, which heighten mood. However, more often than not the motivation to exercise significantly decreases with depression, and sticking with a regimen becomes extremely difficult. Somehow you have to try to visualize how you feel after exercising to try to get yourself out to do it, although this may seem impossible at times. Even if it is all you can do to walk to your mailbox and back, that is a start, and you can build from that. It is important to stay on top of your exercise schedule so that you never get totally out of a routine.

Eating Habits and Supplements

I have also tried to change my eating habits: I eat as few processed foods as possible, and my diet leans more toward healthy, fresh foods. In the past I've incorporated juicing into my lifestyle (when motivated to buy the vegetables and clean the juicer after juicing). I also take vitamin and mineral supplements to achieve optimal cellular nutrition and to give my body its best shot for being healthy. One supplement recommended by my psychiatrist specifically for bipolar is the class of Omega 3 fatty acids (typically taken via fish oil). For each person the amount needed will vary, but Omega 3 promotes healthy functioning of the brain. I have both the desire and need to learn about whatever will go into my body, and I feel this really helps me.

I still struggle with eating habits, particularly during the fall when I seem to crave carbohydrates and then eat more in the evenings than normal; this is something that accompanies SAD. Although I have difficulty controlling my carbohydrate cravings and overeating, just being aware of the reasons why these changes occur is beneficial. I have also learned that keeping busy and limiting what foods are in the house is also helpful; living alone, however, seems to warrant evening emotional eating. I'm still working on that. Weight has always been a struggle for me, and I feel I have to continually work at trying to lose weight, or at the very least maintain the weight I am at. The lithium and Tegretol do not help, because one of the side effects is weight gain. Balancing the right amount of exercise and food consumption for me is a constant battle, but it certainly is obtainable. Given the alternative, the medications have certainly been the better choice to give me a more stable life.

Light Therapy in the Fall and Winter

If you experience SAD, as I do so severely, there are light boxes that provide artificial light when the days are shorter to trick the brain into thinking there is more natural light. Using a light box has been a big help to me, and I now start light therapy in August prior to my bad time, which is the fall, when I feel the effects of the days getting shorter. I use the light in the morning, and it helps with my motivation throughout the day because I am not feeling the effects of the days getting shorter and the lack of natural sunlight as much. For me this typically begins to subside in January, but for many it is not until the beginning of spring when they start to feel back to normal again. Balance is much easier for me when my SAD is under control.

Alcohol Consumption

Nineteen years after diagnosis, I finally learned how alcohol affects me regarding my medication. One consideration that has been shared with me is that my medications and alcohol may compete for metabolism by the liver, and in turn cause the alcohol to stay in my system longer. I had been a social drinker since college, not realizing the intensifying effects alcohol could have had on me due to my medications, specifically the mood stabilizers lithium and Tegretol. I was only informed of this correlation by a psychiatrist in 2003. This metabolism-medication correlation had never been spelled out to me prior to my first clinical depression in 2000. Although I was aware of the depressive effect of alcohol, I did not feel it truly had any significant bearing on my well-being, and I never saw that it affected me in that manner. Perhaps I was in denial up until 2003 and never wanted to be anything but normal to myself and others. Not drinking alcohol would be just one more thing that would make me different from those around me.

After my second major clinical episode of depression in September 2002, I realized there was evidence for potential risk for subsequent depressions. I chose to reevaluate what further lifestyle modifications I could do for my well-being. I actually stopped all alcohol consumption for a while. For the most part, over the next few years I limited my alcohol intake to one, possibly two drinks and not on a regular basis. More important, over time I have become very comfortable with who I am, and the choices I make to stay healthy outweigh the risks associated with alcohol. Also, drinking alcohol really defeats the purpose of taking antidepressants (which I took for several years starting in 2000) because alcohol interacts with the same neurotransmitter system that the antidepressants do, counteracting their function of increasing the levels of serotonin.

Alcohol can also disrupt the regulation of sleep cycles: although it may be easier to fall asleep, our quality of sleep is compromised with alcohol in our system. Sleep deprivation of any kind increases our risk for entering into a manic phase.

Good Support System

Having a good support system in place has been very beneficial to me. My initial support system began with my family and continued throughout my first hospitalization and beyond. During my hospital stays, my mom's everyday visits (interspersed with other family members on many days) had a tremendously positive impact on my newfound uncertainties, and my family's choice to stick by me exemplified their unconditional love and provided comfort to me. In addition, many friends, the pastor of the church I attended, and members of the church would call, visit, and send lots of cards. All of these people contributed to my support system and played a role in my recovery. The other patients in the hospital (as well as some of the nurses and staff) were there for support as well as understanding.

For me, involvement in a local support group for both unipolar and bipolar illnesses (Depression and Bipolar Support Alliance [DBSA]) makes a difference as well. I find much comfort in sharing my experiences with others who have similar mood disorders. I find that each week I attend, the experience can be different: at times I really need to be heard and want advice from others, other times I come with nothing to share but listen and benefit from what is shared, and sometimes I am a support to others. Whatever direction the course of the discussions take, the meetings have been beneficial to me in some way. I also recognize that for me, attending every week does not serve me well, because sometimes it's just too much, and I feel I am trending toward being too close and involved with the illness. It is important to recognize these boundaries.

In addition to organized support groups, it is essential to have someone to talk to one-on-one, such as a friend or family member. I met some people in the hospital with whom I maintained friendships with for quite some time. I also have some very good friends who have bipolar disorder with whom I can talk to, and they understand a lot of what I am going through. My uncle George is always willing to talk, and we share a special bond because of the illness. My immediate family members are empathetic to my illness and have always been very supportive of me, even though they have not experienced bipolar disorder directly.

I also have other friends who do not have the illness, and they listen and can be both sympathetic and compassionate even without totally understanding my illness. Many of these friends have family members or other friends with the illness and seem to have some degree of understanding, but many have no association with the illness. Helping others to understand the illness can also lend itself to alleviate the negativity associated with bipolar disorder.

Whenever possible, I try to avoid those who are not supportive and feel people with bipolar just need to "get over it." If trying to help them understand the illness does not work, it becomes unhealthy to be around them for any length of time. This type of environment increases the potential for more negative feelings and will not aid in the process of becoming well. The pervasive fear of those who do not understand bipolar disorder or who do not desire to understand most likely stems from a general lack of understanding, their preconceived notions, or just plain ignorance.

Research and Self-Education

Since being diagnosed with bipolar disorder, I have spent much time reading a vast number of journal articles and books, and I've utilized the Internet extensively to learn as much as possible about this illness and to stay abreast of the current research that is ongoing. Educating myself has helped me tremendously to understand what I've got and how to best handle and manage it.

Spirituality

I recognize that each individual may have his own sense of spirituality or what it is for him that provides a life context—perhaps a higher power, nature, music, or meditation. For me, it comes from God and through my Christian faith. My faith is a vehicle that helps me achieve a solid foundation that provides a sense of calmness, peacefulness, and patience within myself and with the illness. It also contributes to my desire to persevere.

Over the years enduring this illness, I see how much my spirituality has played a role in keeping me well, or as well as possible, in the midst of my struggles associated with my bipolar disorder. Actually, my faith has helped my overall health both in a physical, mental, and emotional capacity, as it has been a basis for how I choose to manage my illness. In particular, early on in my diagnosis there was fear and anxiety for what would happen to my life as a result of the illness. By having faith and trusting in God, the peace that fills me is truly amazing. The clarity I have found through my relationship with God has been essential for me to live in balance and to sustain a strong sense of well-being in the midst of all the unknowns. My faith is why I respond the way I do to myself, others, and life situations. God has blessed me with the aptitude to deal with this illness and to respond without resentment and bitterness in the midst of suffering and difficulty.

How to Manage When Warning Signs Are Present

I have come to realize that even in the early years during my hospitalizations, I found safety in the hospital. The hospital meant comfort, people like me, and doctors to take care of me. I saw checking into the hospital as my only option. Over the years I learned how important taking time for myself is when I am overwhelmed and experience feelings of stress, anxiety, and negativity toward myself due to life situations. These types of feelings can so easily and quickly begin to shift to spiral down into a depression (or for some, they can spiral up to a mania). Recognizing warning signs helps me to prevent either a manic or depressive episode. My warning signs include changes in stress management or feelings of being overwhelmed, sleep patterns (too much or too little), energy levels (either diminished for days or an overabundance), exercise habits (nonexistent or excessive, including when my motivation for exercising has been depleted), eating habits (consuming too little or too much), desire to withdraw from the world, and irritability. Although many of these are everyday feelings, there is a pattern, and they go hand-in-hand with one another.

Recognizing these warning signs and knowing how to address them are coping skills that have helped me to avoid another hospitalization. When the warning signs begin to present themselves and last for more than a few days, I am in contact with my doctor, and if necessary we make medication changes along with behavioral modifications. By managing my bipolar disorder with the help of my doctors, I have not only kept myself from enduring subsequent hospitalizations, but I've also minimized the severity of my depressions and avoided manias altogether.

It is my thought that by keeping these safeguards and coping skills in place, I should be able to avoid the extremes from here on out. I am also not naïve to the fact that anything could happen with this illness, but at least I've got a better chance by staying mindful.

Afterword
Where I Am Today

DISCOVERING MY OWN STRENGTH and ability to persevere over these past twenty-seven years sometimes astounds me. If I knew what I would be up against, both within me as well as the inaccurate assumptions about mental illness by others, facing all the challenges at once would have proved to be too daunting. I do consider myself to be fortunate in that the challenges came in pieces or steps as I continued to mature. In order for me to not be consumed with what this illness does to affect my personality, I have to constantly remind myself to concentrate on where I am today and focus on that.

For me, my overriding belief is that even the most difficult challenges of my bipolar disorder will eventually pass, even in the bleakest of times. This is due to my continued character development, support from family and friends, general awareness, education, competent psychiatrists, and most importantly my faith. I have come a long way since being diagnosed, and the only thing I know for sure is that my hope will not leave me. I know things will not always be easy, but I also know that I will always be okay at some point, even if it takes a little while and a lot of commitment to get there. Of course, I realize there are no guarantees for what the future holds for me with respect to this illness.

How I have chosen to respond to this illness has had a fundamental impact. When I believed I was damaged, I was damaged. Now that I believe I am not damaged, I am not damaged. Whatever I believe about myself is ultimately what becomes true. For me, achieving a state of true integrity in belief, word, and action allows for self-reliance. Believing in my own ability to be consistent in my values raises me up to a place of confidence. For this reason I know I do not have to live in fear. The absence of fear creates freedom in living because I'm no longer troubled by what others think of me in regard to my illness.

I do acknowledge my perseverance, strength, and resilience in dealing with this illness. For the most part, since my twenties I have had to deal with it on my own. I certainly have always had support from family, friends, and mental health professionals, but I have not had someone with me consistently throughout my ups and downs, such as a spouse. So many people who have this illness have told me that they could have never made it without their spouse. I'm quite sure being married to the right person could be a great help when it comes to support. I also see how if one is not with the right person, life can be much worse in regard to this illness. I have managed on my own, and I do know this is possible for others. Even as I say I have done this mostly on my own, it is important to note that I certainly do not feel alone in this illness, and for me that began in the very beginning, when I was first hospitalized. I was surrounded by others who shared similar illnesses, and we certainly interacted a lot while we were there twenty-four hours a day. Even then, I knew I was not the only one, and that made a difference that has remained with me.

Focusing on where I am today enables me to continue to move forward knowing that bipolar disorder is not predictable. Since completing the earlier chapters, I have started to experience depressions (stemming from SAD) that have been different in a way than previously known to me. These depressions last longer and are more intense. I view myself through a very critical lens and find it hard to accept the depression is totally out of my control. Much of these months I did not feel like the real me. I was living in a paradox: others' perceptions told me I was usually doing a little better than I thought I was (the deception of the depression), but at the same time I was struggling to fight to do what I could to function (the thievery of the depression). I wanted to be who they thought I was, but the depression was telling me otherwise and took away my full capabilities.

Only when the depressions would lift would I be able to recognize how insidious the depressions were and what a powerful grip they had on me. They depleted my true identity, but when I would come out of them, I regained my old sense of self again. Such an unsettling dynamic! I have to believe that one day I will conquer this part of my illness with the right combination of medications and lifestyle modifications—perhaps we just haven't found that magical combination for me yet. I'm certainly not ready to accept that this is it for me for five months out of the year.

Following my most recent bout of depression, new beginnings and big possibilities arose: I was given the option to request a severance package from my sales job of ten years, which offered me the opportunity to pursue a long-awaited goal of working in mental health advocacy. At first the choices and chances seemed slim; I had found just three mental health advocacy jobs to apply to over a period of six months. Even though I had my finances in order and knew the severance was going to sustain me for quite some time, the reality of not having a secure job scared me. I *really* desired both gainful and satisfying employment.

I interviewed for one of those three positions I applied for, and after two interviews I was offered the job. I started my new position as wellness and recovery manager for mental health and substance abuse at a behavioral healthcare division in the Washington, DC, area. The crux of this job is to help to support the shift of the division's current culture to a more recovery-oriented system of care and to demonstrate that recovery is possible for all individuals, with the knowledge that the recovery aspect is different for each person. This newly created position seemed to fit my background and qualifications perfectly, and it also required that the person has, or has been, a recipient of mental health or substance abuse services. This requirement, which would allow the perspective of someone with "lived experience" in a management position, showed me the level of commitment they had to helping others with their recovery. Meaningful employment proves to be rewarding. This is a new feeling for me.

By taking a chance on myself to explore a new career path, I continue to live out the meaning of hope with this illness. Life is continuously fresh and new. "I am not my illness" continues to resound.

Living with bipolar disorder for twenty-seven years has deepened characteristics within me that were there before but have since broadened to another level. My empathy and compassion are now central to who I have become. My respect for others and for people's differences has increased considerably. I am very mindful not to make assumptions about others and their levels of suffering, and not just about mental illness; just because something looks a certain way does not mean the reality in front of me is the whole story.

As much as I have struggled throughout my adult life with my bipolar disorder, I have also grown as a person. I've grown up with it, and it's a part of me. I've struggled with it, and yet I've still embraced it. I feel it has helped to shape me into a better person, and I know I can make a difference for others because of my response to it.

Appendix 1
Bipolar Disorder Explained

BIPOLAR DISORDER IS A misunderstood illness affecting 5.7 million adults in the United States.[1] Too many people go undiagnosed for many years while experiencing symptoms. The average delay for accurate diagnosis is ten years.[2]

Bipolar disorder (also referred to as manic depression) is an illness of the brain thought to be due to a chemical imbalance. This imbalance affects mood and, by default, cognitive and rational thinking. Mood is reflected in the extremes known as mania (highs that can include reckless and exuberant behavior) and depression (lows that can include despair and even tragically result in suicide). Many people express the symptoms of the illness in milder forms on the spectrum between the extremes.

It can be very difficult for someone without a mental illness to comprehend that mood is subject to a chemical imbalance. Regarding the mania, it's not necessarily about someone being happy, irritable, or dangerous, but the chemical imbalance itself causes a person to feel and behave these ways. The manic episodes are often a really good feeling and may escalate to psychosis, where the person could experience auditory and visual hallucinations as well as grandiose ideas. The depression is not necessarily only about being sad, as many would think. Clinical depression also stems from this chemical imbalance in the brain, which causes the person to have feelings of sadness, irritability, and worthlessness that can affect behavior. The depressed person will typically lack the ability to concentrate, will not find interest in things one was previously interested in, and have difficulty maintaining routine sleep. It is important to note that both mania and depression can be triggered by events (often stressful), but sometimes it happens on its own, without warning.

Once in a full-blown manic or depressed state, stopping the process in its tracks on one's own is extremely difficult, if not impossible. As time goes by, however, and if one is able to recognize the warning signs, one can often prevent a full-blown episode of mania or depression, or at least make it be less severe.

There are different types of bipolar disorder. The most common are type I and type II. Typical characteristics of bipolar type I include the extreme euphoric highs (mania) and the deep lows of depression. Often the depression follows the high, but it does not have to occur in this sequence. Milder forms of the extremes can also be experienced; these mild manias are referred to as hypomania. Mild depression is just that—a mild or lighter form of depression. Bipolar type II involves predominantly depressive episodes with some episodes of hypomania. There are other variations of bipolar disorder that can be found in the *DSM-IV,* the diagnostic criteria manual for psychiatric illnesses.

It is important to note that the recovery process and aftereffects of a manic or depressed episode can be extremely difficult. Often the behavior in these episodes can be embarrassing, damaging, or alienating. Relationships may need to be repaired, and some relationships can be destroyed. The person needs time to put the pieces back into place, to regain others' trust, and to accept the losses. There is also the healing process that goes along with the rebuilding of one's sense of self while also working on achieving a sense of wellness.

Although genetics play a key role in bipolar disorder and knowing family history is very important, there is no diagnostic test for it. Diagnosis is based on symptoms and behaviors and often comes with an abrupt and heightened change in behavior. These behaviors are often misunderstood and viewed as unacceptable in a rational society. Environmental triggers often contribute to the initial onset of manic or depressive episodes.

Presently there is no known cure for bipolar disorder. Managing this illness is the only option and requires the conscious decision to take action toward wellness (much like the management of diabetes or hypertension). When a person with bipolar disorder accepts the illness and takes steps toward adherence with his or her treatment, this illness has great potential to be managed. It is not easy, but it is certainly possible.

Each person diagnosed with bipolar disorder will react differently to medications and treatment plans, and not everyone achieves the same outcomes (or has the same access to resources). Denial about having this illness often occurs, and usually serves only to prevent a person from moving forward in a balanced manner. However, for many of the millions diagnosed with bipolar disorder, living a productive life is achievable.

Appendix 2
Lithium

LITHIUM'S HEALING PROPERTIES WERE utilized even before it was scientifically documented, as lithium is a naturally occurring element in nature (found in mineral rocks, natural brines, mineral waters, and in some plant, animal, and human tissues).[1] Even before the properties of lithium were scientifically studied, in the second century the Greek physician Soranus of Ephesus advised his patients suffering from manic insanity and melancholia to take in "natural waters" from baths that appeared to have healing properties. These "natural waters" were alkaline springs rich in lithium.[2] The lithium compound was only later identified in 1817 and recognized in the periodic table of elements (the 1A group of alkaline metals), and it was so named because it was found in stone (*lithos* in Greek).[3]

In the mid-nineteenth century, lithium compounds were studied as a treatment for gout and the dissolution of kidney stones, but this scientific work was unsuccessful. Approximately one century later, the use of lithium was given as a salt substitute for patients with heart disease and high blood pressure because these ailments require low-sodium diets. The results were devastating because lithium can be toxic in low concentrations, and several patients actually died from toxicity. Lithium usage was still in its testing phase, and lithium chloride as a salt substitute for sodium chloride had not yet been approved by the Federal Drug Administration. Needless to say, the negative press these studies received made people wary of the lithium drug compound.[4]

In 1949, Australian psychiatrist John F. Cade reintroduced lithium for its healing properties for the treatment of bipolar disorder. Cade published studies that revealed lithium's antimanic properties, thereby being credited for the discovery of its therapeutic effects in treating bipolar disorder as a biological condition rather than emotional.[5] Rather than receiving wide acclaim, Cade's study went largely unnoticed because psychoanalytical study at this time, following World War II, was undergoing many changes. In Germany, psychiatric researchers and clinicians were under scrutiny. In the United States and England, the study of psychiatry turned its focus on talk therapy (rather than biological etiology) for mental health distress. Those who showed severity in mental health symptoms too difficult to control were routinely diagnosed as schizophrenic and put into an institution.[6] There was little, if any, middle ground for any other form of mental illness diagnosis. Additionally, in the United States lithium had "a very bad reputation among physicians, and it was another factor that explains the delay in the acceptance of Cade's discovery of lithium's efficacy in bipolar disorder."[7]

In the 1950s Morgans Schou, a Danish psychiatrist, published research studies that supported Cade's discoveries, once again bringing lithium back into consideration for the treatment of bipolar disorder.[8] Schou was an advocate of the effectiveness of lithium in treating both acute mania as well as its ability to prevent other manifestations of bipolar disorder. Schou spent much time proving to his colleagues that lithium would not only have an effect on acute symptoms of mania, but it would also have an effect on the recurrence of symptoms, and hence the illness. As more patients used lithium for treatment, Schou and a British colleague, Paul Baalstrup, conducted the British study, "Lithium as a Prophylactic Agent: Its Effect against Recurrent Depressions and Manic-Depressive Psychosis."[9] Their study concluded that lithium did indeed affect bipolar disorder. One feature of their study stood out as most impressive: it was a double-blind, controlled study, meaning they utilized their patients with bipolar disorder who had been stable on their medication (lithium) for at least one year. After dividing their patients into two equal groups, one group's lithium was replaced with a placebo. Of the thirty-nine patients whose lithium was substituted with placebo, twenty-one relapsed within five months; of the forty-five patients whose lithium was not substituted, none relapsed.[10]

Ronald Fieve, MD, advocated highly for lithium's effectiveness for manic-depressive illness among American physicians in the 1970s.[11] Over the last several decades, however, practitioners have still required lithium usage to prove its credibility for the treatment of acute mania and acute bipolar depression.

Even today, lithium appears to be underutilized regardless of its efficacy as a mood stabilizer. Lithium has been prescribed for the treatment of bipolar disorder for decades, but it is not promoted by pharmaceutical companies as much as the newer classes of medications available. How much this may play a role in its use by prescribing doctors is an unknown factor.

Although my lithium dosage has slowly decreased over time, it continues to be the fundamental medication that plays a major role in achieving my mental health wellness.

Notes

Chapter 4: My Little Corner of Hell: Hospitalization #3
1. Frederick K. Goodwin, MD, and Kay Redfield Jamison, PhD, *Manic-Depressive Illness: Bipolar Disorders and Recurrent Depression, 2nd ed.* (New York: Oxford University Press, Inc., 2007), 815.

Chapter 7: Opening Pandora's Box: Introduction to Depression
1. Accutane [package insert]. Nutley, NJ: Roche Laboratories, Inc., 2005.

Chapter 9: Wanting the Pain to Go Away: Suicide
1. Substance Abuse and Mental Health Services Administration News Release. "First-of-a-Kind National Study Reveals that 8.3 Million Adults in the U.S. had Serious Thoughts of Committing Suicide in the Past Year," September 17, 2009, accessed September 09, 2010, http://www.samhsa.gov/newsroom/advisories/090917suicide0907.aspx.
2. American Foundation for Suicide Prevention. "Facts and Figures: National Statistics," 2009, accessed May 15, 2012, http://www.afsp.org/index.cfm?fuseaction=home.viewpage&page_id=050fea9f-b064-4092-b1135c3a70de1fda.
3. Centers for Disease Control (US Public Health Service). "Suicide: Risk and Protective Factors," reviewed August 31, 2010, accessed May 19, 2012, http://www.cdc.gov/ViolencePrevention/suicide/riskprotectivefactors.html.

4. Ibid.
5. Goodwin and Jamison, 967–71.
6. Kay Redfield Jamison, PhD, *Night Falls Fast: Understanding Suicide* (New York: Alfred A. Knopf, 1999), 39.

Chapter 12: Fearing Rejection: Dating Relationships
1. Conversation with Glenn J. Treisman, MD, PhD, Psychiatry and Behavioral Sciences, Johns Hopkins School of Medicine, Baltimore, MD.

Chapter 14: Family Connections: Genetic Predisposition
1   National Alliance on Mental Illness. "Dual Diagnosis and Integrated Treatment of Mental Illness and Substance Abuse Disorder," September 2003, accessed May 17, 2012, http://www.nami .org/Template.cfm?Section=By_Illness&Template=/TaggedPage/ TaggedPageDisplay.cfm&TPLID=54&ContentID=23049.
2. Kimberlee Hose, "Premenstrual Dysphoric Disorder," 2003, accessed December 21, 2006, http://www.healthyplace.com/ communities/depression/pmdd.asp.
3. Ibid.
4. *The Free Dictionary Online*, "Catatonic Schizophrenia," accessed May 20, 2012, http://the freedictionary.com/ catatonic+schizophrenia.
5. Francis Mark Mondimore, *Bipolar Disorder: A Guide for Patients and Families* (Baltimore: Johns Hopkins University Press, 1999), 128.

Appendix 1: Bipolar Disorder Explained
1. National Institutes of Mental Health, "Bipolar Disorder Among Adults," June 2005, accessed May 30, 2012, http://www.nimh. nih.gov/statistics/1BIPOLAR_ADULT.shtml.
2. National Alliance on Mental Illness, "Understanding Bipolar Disorder and Recovery," August 2008, accessed May 17, 2012, http:// www.nami.org/Template.cfm?Section=By_Illness&template=/ ContentManagement/ContentDisplay.cfm&ContentID=67728.

Appendix 2: Lithium
1. Ronald R. Fieve, MD, *Moodswing: The Third Revolution in*

Psychiatry (New York: Bantam Books, 1975), 208.

2. Anastase Georgotas and Samuel Gershon, "Historical Perspectives and Current Highlights on Lithium Treatment in Manic-Depressive Illness," *Journal of Clinical Psychology 1*, no. 1 (1981), 27–31. From Mondimore, *Bipolar Disorder*, 261.

3. Fieve, 208.

4. Mondimore, 85.

5. Mondimore, 70.

6. Ibid.

7. Mondimore, 87.

8. Mondimore, 85.

9. Paul Baalstrup and Morgan Schou, "Lithium as a Prophylactic Agent: Its Effect against Recurrent Depressions and Manic-Depressive Psychosis," *Archives of General Psychiatry 16*, no.2 (1967), 162–72. From Mondimore, *Bipolar Disorder*, 85.

10. Mondimore, 86–87.

11. Mondimore, 71.

Resources

American Foundation for Suicide Prevention (AFSP)
120 Wall Street, Twenty-Ninth Floor
New York, NY 10005
Toll-free: 1.888.333.2377
www.afsp.org

bp Magazine: Hope and Harmony for People with Bipolar
www.bphope.com

Depression and Bipolar Support Alliance (DBSA)
730 N. Franklin Street, Suite 501
Chicago, IL 60654-7225
Toll-free: 1.800.826.3632
www.dbsalliance.org

National Alliance on Mental Illness (NAMI)
3803 N. Fairfax Drive, Suite 100
Arlington, VA 22203
703.524.7600
www.nami.org

National Institute of Mental Health (NIMH)
6001 Executive Boulevard
Bethesda, MD 20892-9663
301.443.4513
Toll-free: 1.866.615.6464
www.nimh.nih.gov
http://mentalhealth.gov/health/publications/bipolar-disorder
/complete-index.shtml (specific information on bipolar disorder)

Substance Abuse and Mental Health Services Association
(SAMHSA)
1 Choke Cherry Road
Rockville, MD 20857
Toll-free: 1.877.SAMHSA.7 (1.877.726.4727)
www.samhsa.gov

National Suicide Prevention Lifeline
Toll-free: 1.800.273.8255
www.suicidepreventionlifeline.org

Websites and Blogs That Are Helpful to Me

www.bipolarhappens.com — Julie A. Fast
www.bipoaradvantage.com — Tom Wooton

Acknowledgments

I COULD NOT POSSIBLY individually name all the people who have supported me along the way with this project: my family, friends, coworkers, support group members, former customers, and mental health advocates. There are also people who gave me great encouragement whom I met at various conferences, as well as those I have met in random places, such as airports and restaurants. Finding hundreds of people who have connections to this illness and who expressed interest in this book gave me more motivation to complete this project. I always knew I would finish it, but I could not envision how I would get there and how long it would take. It has truly been a labor of love.

My deepest thanks to the following:

My very talented editor and dear friend, Kimberly Tyler, who believed in me from day one. She now knows me more than most and accepts me as I am. Always compassionate and empathetic, she learned how an illness like this can affect a person's life. She believes in the importance of sharing my story with people who have a connection to mental health challenges, either directly or indirectly. She has supported me 100 percent and has given me strength and encouragement to make this dream a reality. This book would not be what it is today without her help and dedication to such an important subject matter.

Dr. Frederick K. Goodwin, who has been a very important part of my writing process. After getting to know me and understanding the nature of my writing, he later agreed to write the foreword. He was actively involved in my work and always believed in me. I am grateful for the time he dedicated to reviewing multiple drafts of my manuscript and providing valuable feedback to help to make this book the best it could be. I have great regard for him, not only because he is a leading expert in the field of psychiatry and a major contributor to the research of bipolar disorder, but also because he is a very understanding and empathetic person.

My peer who so openly and willingly shared her story with her extreme depression and her struggles with bipolar disorder. By sharing her story, she helped me to be able to include something that is often a very crucial component of this illness, but one that I have not experienced. I am very grateful to her for this.

Amy Sutter, for reviewing the manuscript and providing valuable feedback and comments.

Julie Fast, for her support, expert advice, and friendship throughout this process.

Dr. Thomas Wise and Pete Earley, for their belief in my story and their encouragement.

My immediate family, who have always supported me with this project, and to Uncle George, who was willing to share his story and who has been a big support to me over the years.

And to Jim, who found out about this project (and that I have this illness) the day he met me. He knew very little about bipolar disorder, and he still chose to get to know me for me; the illness was secondary. He has never seen me and the illness as one. He has supported, encouraged, and accepted me with all that comes with an illness of this sort, both the very good and the challenging times. I recognize it is not always easy, yet our relationship is steadfast. I certainly love you.

Thank you to all of these very important people in my life, and especially to God, without whom I am nothing.

CPSIA information can be obtained at www.ICGtesting.com
Printed in the USA
BVOW011144121112

305304BV00003B/1/P

9 781475 949803